The mission of Storey Publishing is to serve our customers by publishing practical information that encourages personal independence in harmony with the environment.

Edited by Deanna F. Cook and Lisa Hiley

Art direction and book design by Jessica Armstrong

Text production by Erin Dawson

Indexed by Nancy D. Wood

Cover photography by © Carl Tremblay, front and back (mason jars, except center); Mars Vilaubi, back (mason jar, center); © sdominick/iStockphoto.com, back (young scientist)

Interior photography by © Carl Tremblay, with Mars Vilaubi, 25 bottom, 27 top, 30, 31, 47 top, 60, 66, 82 bottom, 86, 93 right, 114 top, 115, 122 left

Additional photography by © badahos/Shutterstock, 52; © Buyenlarge/Getty Images, 42; © Dafinchi/Shutterstock, 32 bottom; © Donna Griffith, www.donnagriffith.com, 83; © Hajakely/iStockphoto.com, 75 bottom; © HandmadePictures/iStockphoto.com, 26 far left; © JHVEPhoto/iStockphoto.com, 97; © Kelly Nelson/Alamy Stock Photo, 88 hummingbird; © LynGianni/iStockphoto.com, 73 top; © m-kojot/iStockphoto.com, 29 bottom; © Minerva Studio/Shutterstock, 59 bottom; © no-limit-pictures/iStockphoto.com, 47 bottom; © xalanx/iStockphoto.com, 61 bottom; © robvann/iStockphoto.com, 57; © Steve Bower /Shutterstock, 17 right; © Todd Bannor/Alamy Stock Photo, 87 inset

Illustrations by Andy Smith

© 2018 by Jonathan Adolph

Storey Publishing
210 MASS MoCA Way
North Adams, MA 01247
storey.com

PRINTED IN CHINA THROUGH ASIA PACIFIC OFFSET

10   9   8   7   6   5   4   3   2   1

Library of Congress Cataloging-in-Publication Data

Title: Mason jar science : 40 slimy, squishy, super-cool experiments / Jonathan Adolph.
Description: North Adams, MA : Storey Publishing, [2018] | Audience: Ages 8-12. | Includes index.
Identifiers: LCCN 2017061052 (print) | LCCN 2017061608 (ebook) | ISBN 9781612129877 (ebook) | ISBN 9781612129860 (hardcover : alk. paper)
Subjects: LCSH: Science—Experiments—Juvenile literature. | Science Projects—Juvenile literature.
Classification: LCC Q164 (ebook) | LCC Q164 .A346 2018 (print) | DDC 507.8—dc23
LC record available at https://lccn.loc.gov/2017061052

Be sure to read all instructions carefully before beginning your experiments and follow the safety warnings while conducting them. Use only the specific ingredients listed for best and safest results. Adult supervision is required for some projects.

MASON ★ JAR
SCIENCE

40 Slimy, Squishy, Super-Cool Experiments

JONATHAN ADOLPH

Storey Publishing

For my father, Ron Adolph, a man of science

ACKNOWLEDGMENTS

Scientific achievement is generally a team effort, and so it was with this book. Thank you to the folks at Storey who made it all happen, especially Deanna Cook, Lisa Hiley, and Jessica Armstrong. Thank you, Tim Martin, for your close reading and scientific expertise. And, finally, thank you, Sarah, for appreciating my compulsion to fill our kitchen windowsills with sweet potato vines, avocado trees, dripping stalactites, shell-less eggs, weightlifting beans, and grass-haired men. Every mad scientist needs an understanding assistant.

Science is the key to our future, and if you don't believe in science, then you're holding everybody back.

— Bill Nye the Science Guy

CONTENTS

THE MAGIC OF CHEMISTRY

15

EARTH SCIENCE
for Earthlings

39

The Root of All Fun BOTANY

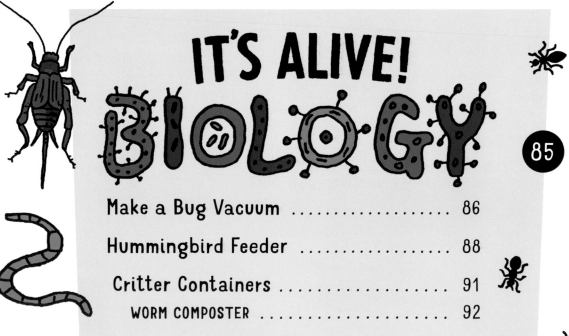

IT'S ALIVE! BIOLOGY

UNDERSTANDING MATTER IN MOTION
PHYSICS 107

WHAT'S SO GREAT ABOUT SCIENCE?

Do you ever wonder how people came up with the amazing things that make our lives so interesting? Things like airplanes, televisions, and computers, or even ice cream? Think about it. Someone had to figure out that stirring milk and sugar while freezing the mixture at the same time makes a creamy dessert that's not solid but not liquid, either. How did they do that? Was the invention of ice cream just plain luck?

Nope.

It was science.

That's right, the very same science you study in school.

Science is more than just a bunch of things you have to know for a class. It's a way of thinking. It's a whole system for making sense of the world, one that we humans have relied on for thousands of years. It uses something called the scientific method (see page 12), which lets us figure things out by doing tests and looking at evidence.

Before we had science, people came up with all sorts of crazy answers to tricky questions such as *Why do people get sick? Why does the sun rise?* And even, *What can we eat for dessert?*

Science lets us look at mysteries and then use reason and experiments to solve them. And the more we humans understand, the more we can achieve. That's how science has given us all of our amazing inventions and discoveries, from the very first wheel to the latest smart phone.

But you don't have to be a researcher, professor, or inventor to experience the thrills of science. Anyone can do it. All it takes is curiosity, a plan of action, and a few supplies.

Equipped with his five senses, man explores the universe around him and calls the adventure Science.

— *Edwin Powell Hubble, astronomer*

WHY MASON JARS?

In the movies, scientists work in high-tech laboratories crammed with glass beakers, bubbling flasks, and fancy display cases that show off their collections of meteorites and dinosaur skeletons.

But that's Hollywood, where they can afford all that stuff. Here in the real world, we like to do science with supplies that are inexpensive, don't easily break, and that you probably already have on hand. That's why we love mason jars, which are designed for processing food at high heat and preserving it for a long time.

They come in all sizes and styles, from tiny 4-ounce jelly jars to huge half-gallon juice jars. To do the experiments in this book, you'll need mostly half-pint, pint, and quart jars (check the materials list given with each experiment). Here's how they compare to real scientific equipment.

The Mason Jar Versus . . .

The beaker. This container with a spout is used for heating and mixing liquids. Mason jars, which are designed to hold hot foods, are also heat proof.

The graduated cylinder. The measurements on the side allow a scientist to precisely measure a liquid. Many mason jars also have helpful measuring lines.

The flask. The narrow neck lets scientists swirl liquids without spilling them, and carry them around the lab. Mason jars have screw-on lids that let you do the same.

And that's just in the chemistry lab . . . with mason jars you can do experiments in biology (study live bugs!), earth science (make stalactites!), and botany (grow plants!). We'll even show you how to turn them into cool scientific instruments.

Let's get started!

flask

beaker

graduated cylinder

mason jar

measuring lines

Using the SCIENTIFIC METHOD to Solve Mysteries

Have you ever come across something weird or unusual and thought, What's up with that? If you are the curious type (and we suspect that you are), you'll want to know more. You could try guessing, or making up an explanation that sounds good. But scientists have found a better way to get at the truth, using experiments to gather evidence and draw conclusions. It's called the scientific method, and it works something like this . . .

Start with a question . . .

That's weird! I wonder why that is?

You see something odd, or something happens that leaves you puzzled, or you're just curious about why something is the way it is. And so you start wondering *What's going on?*

Draw a conclusion

Based on your tests, try to come up with a conclusion that explains what you observed. And then get ready to think some more. Because every conclusion raises new questions. The work of science is never over. That's why it's such a powerful tool for understanding. It forces us to keep asking questions and to keep seeking evidence for our answers. And by doing that, it helps us discover more about the universe.

I think I have an idea . . .

You give it some more thought. Maybe you do some research, and because you are pretty smart, you come up with a possible explanation. Scientists call this a hypothesis. Now comes the part that makes science more than just one person's hunch.

Try to prove it

You need to prove that your thinking is correct, which means coming up with some kind of test, or experiment, that gives you solid evidence. Here's where scientists show how creative they can be (think of Galileo dropping various balls from the leaning tower of Pisa to show that objects fall at the same speed)!

Learn from success — and failure

What? Your experiment didn't work out the way you expected? That's great! Because failure can also give you important information. So keep coming up with new experiments that can tell you even more.

Get a reality check

Did your test show you were right? To be sure, have someone else try to replicate it (meaning repeat it and get the same results). Were the results not what you expected? Maybe you need to revise your thinking. Ask others for feedback, do some more research, or look again at what you've done. Maybe your "failures" are actually telling you something important!

THE MAGIC OF CHEMISTRY

What is all the stuff on Earth made from, and how can we make new stuff from it? Chemistry is the field of science that helps us find out. Humans have probably been asking this since we first discovered fire (a chemical reaction!), and over the centuries we've used chemistry to create the incredible world we live in today. It gave us our first metal tools and the latest disease-curing drugs. It lets us grow more food, create high-tech computers, and send people into outer space.

But chemistry is also something we use every day, when we blend up a smoothie or wash our hands with soap. The following experiments let you see this remarkable science in action. Prepare to be amazed.

LAVA LAMP 2.0

Bubbles and blobs make for a mesmerizing reaction.

If you ask your grandparents about the original lava lamp, they just might get a faraway look in their eyes thinking about the groovy days of the 1960s. But if you want to really blow their minds, show them this simplified version and explain the science behind it. It all comes down to a scientific principle demonstrated every day by the salad dressing in your fridge: oil and water don't mix.

MATERIALS

Pint-size (or larger) mason jar
  with two-piece lid*

Water

Food coloring

Vegetable oil

Effervescent antacid tablets
  (such as Alka-Seltzer)

A larger jar gives more dramatic results.

INSTRUCTIONS

1 Fill the jar about a quarter full with water. Stir in 10 or so drops of food coloring.

2 Add twice as much oil as water, so the jar is three-quarters full.

3 Drop in half of an antacid tablet and observe the reaction.

SCIENCE IN REAL LIFE

When oil spills in the ocean, clean-up crews use floating barriers to keep the oil slick contained. They can do this because the oil is floating on the water's surface, just like the oil in this lava lamp.

What to Watch For

The tablet should start to bubble, causing blobs of colored water to rise up into the oil. Once the initial bubbling slows down, watch as smaller bubbles continue to rise and fall, or add more antacid, broken into smaller chunks.

When you are done, let the jar sit uncovered for a while so all the gas can escape. (Trapping that gas in the jar could cause it to crack!) Store the jar with the lid on, and keep some antacid tablets handy, so you can use your lamp on another groovy day.

What's Going On

The original lava lamp used heat to send mesmerizing blobs of wax rising and falling. Here, we use the gassy fizz from an effervescent antacid tablet. The oil is less dense than the colored water so it floats in a layer on top (for more on density, see Tower of Liquids, page 110). The blobs of water are carried to the surface by the rising carbon dioxide bubbles, and then sink back down when the bubbles reach the top.

SPEAK like a SCIENTIST

A material that bubbles or foams from escaping gas is called effervescent. Antacid tablets are effervescent in the same way that baking soda is when you mix it with an acid such as vinegar. In fact, the tablets actually contain baking soda (sodium bicarbonate) along with citric acid, so when the tablet is dissolved in water, you see a similar reaction: lots of bubbles of carbon dioxide gas. (See Take It Further, page 104.)

WATER FIREWORKS

Set off an explosion of color.

This project lets you detonate bursts of color without having to worry about burning down your house or blowing off a finger! These fireworks don't use fire at all. Just the opposite: water, along with oil and your favorite shades of food coloring.

MATERIALS

Quart-size mason jar

Half-pint mason jar

Room-temperature water

2 ounces vegetable oil

Food coloring

Fork

INSTRUCTIONS

1 Fill the quart jar with room-temperature water, leaving about an inch of space at the top.

2 Pour the vegetable oil into the half-pint jar. Add several drops of food coloring, in various shades.

3 Run the fork gently through the oil a couple times to break the drops of coloring into smaller drops. Don't over mix! Some drops can be big and others can be small.

4 Add the oil mixture to the water jar by slowly pouring it against the side of the jar so the oil floats on the surface of the water, holding all the blobs of food coloring.

What to Watch For

Within 30 seconds or so, the drops of food coloring will fall out of the oil and into the water, leaving trails of color as they sink.

What's Going On

Food coloring doesn't dissolve in oil, so at first it sits on the surface of the water, held by the oil. Eventually, though, it drops through the oil and hits the layer of water below. Once it does, the dye quickly dissolves and you get to admire the colorful result!

WIDE WORLD OF SLIMES

A FIELD GUIDE TO MAKING CRAZY CONCOCTIONS

Who doesn't love slimes, goos, and doughs? Gather a few ordinary ingredients, stir them together (or heat them), and before your eyes they transform into gooey blobs, gross slimes, or moldable clays! But in addition to being just plain fun, these concoctions are great examples of the marvels of chemistry. Each mixture feels and acts the way it does because certain chemical ingredients make it behave that way. Once you know how that chemistry works, you can invent the slime of your dreams! So choose your goo and start concocting!

SLIME

PLAY CLAY

GOO

GOO

Also known as GACK, this smooth, rubbery material can be stretched and squished.

MATERIALS

Pint-size mason jar with two-piece lid

4 ounces white glue

1 teaspoon baking soda

Paint stirrer or other mixing tool

1 tablespoon contact lens solution*

5 or so drops of food coloring

Look for a brand that contains boric acid.

INSTRUCTIONS

1 Pour the glue into the mason jar.

2 Add the baking soda and stir to combine thoroughly. Add the food coloring and stir to combine. (Check out the variations on page 22. Add any extra ingredients now.)

3 Add the contact lens solution and start stirring. Now comes the amazing part. The mixture will become harder to stir, and a blob will start to form around your stirrer as the substances react to form the goo.

4 Keep stirring the blob, or knead your goo with your hands. If it's too sticky, add a ¼ teaspoon more contact lens solution. Adjusting the amounts of glue and lens solution will give you goos of varying consistencies. The more lens solution, the firmer your final goo, but don't overdo it or your goo can become too stiff to stretch.

Stored in the jar with the lid on, your goo should keep for months.

What's Going On

Glue is a polymer, which means it is made up of long chains of molecules. Think of the chains as being like cooked spaghetti noodles, all facing the same way, easily sliding back and forth.

The boric acid in the lens solution combines with the baking soda (sodium bicarbonate) to make borate, a substance that triggers a reaction called cross-linking. When a polymer is cross-linked, all of those chains tangle up into a blob of molecules, sort of like adding thick cheese sauce to the spaghetti and giving it a stir.

21

GOO VARIATIONS!

Multicolored Goo

If you mix up goo in several colors and then twist them together, you'll have made the latest rage in homemade concoctions. Its name: Unicorn Poop.

Glitter Goo

For a more interesting look, stir in some glitter or use glow-in-the-dark paint instead of food coloring (but be careful using the goo on wood or fabric surfaces where it could leave a stain!).

Fluffy Goo

For fluffier goo, add about 2 ounces — a few squirts — of foamy shaving cream (not gel) to the glue and baking soda mixture, and stir it in.

SLIME

This substance, also known as FLUBBER, is similar to goo, but it's more stretchy, less solid, and more slimy! When first made, it has a stringy, snotlike consistency (gross!). Keep it away from anything it might stick to, like carpets, sweaters, and hair!

MATERIALS

- Quart-size mason jar with two-piece lid
- 4 ounces white glue
- 4 ounces water
- 10 or so drops of food coloring
- 4 ounces Sta-Flo liquid starch*
- Paint stirrer or other mixing tool

*This brand contains sodium tetraborate, which is a key ingredient. If you can't find it in the supermarket laundry aisle, you can order it online. Many laundry detergents, including Gain and Tide, also have this ingredient and can be used similarly.

INSTRUCTIONS

1 Combine the glue, water, and food coloring in the jar, and mix with the stirrer.

2 Slowly pour in the starch, stirring it into the other ingredients. The liquid will quickly form a blob. Knead it to firm it up.

Stored in the jar with the lid on, your slime should keep for months.

What's Going On

Sta-Flo liquid starch contains sodium tetraborate, which acts like the boric acid and baking soda in goo to cross-link the polymers in the glue to form slime. Other ingredients in the starch make the slime more squishy and stretchy. You can adjust the sliminess by adding less water or less laundry starch to the glue.

Glitter Slime

Sparkle up your slime by adding a few spoonfuls of glitter to the glue and water mixture in step 1.

Microwave
PLAY CLAY

You can sculpt this soft play dough just like the store-bought version. Left out to dry, it will eventually harden.

MATERIALS

Quart-size mason jar with two-piece lid

Half-pint mason jar

Paint stirrer or other mixing tool

1 cup flour

½ cup salt

1 teaspoon cream of tartar (found in the supermarket spice section)

1 cup water

10 to 15 drops of food coloring

1 teaspoon vegetable oil

INSTRUCTIONS

1 Combine the flour, salt, and cream of tartar in the quart jar and stir.

2 Combine the water and food coloring in the half-pint jar and then pour the liquid into the dry ingredients in the quart jar.

3 Add the oil and stir thoroughly. The mixture should look like very thick paint.

4 Microwave the jar for about 1½ minutes.

5 Using potholders, remove the hot jar, place it on the counter, and give it a quick stir. The clay should have started to solidify. (If it is still liquid, microwave it for another 10 seconds or so.)

6 Let it cool for a minute or so, or until you can comfortably hold the jar, and continue stirring. The mixture should be thick like mud.

7 Scrape it out of the jar onto a surface with a little flour on it and knead it until it's smooth.

Store the clay in the quart jar but let it cool completely before putting on the lid, so water does not condense on the jar's sides. It should keep for months.

SAFETY FIRST: Test the inside of the clay with your fingers to make sure it is cool enough to handle before you start kneading it. It will be hot coming out of the microwave and could burn your hands.

What's Going On

Like bread dough, this play clay is mostly a mixture of flour and water. The other ingredients keep it from getting moldy and help give it a springy texture. Heating the mixture in the microwave (or slowly in a pan on the stove top) helps combine all the ingredients.

Unlike goo or slime, play clay can be molded and holds its shape. Sculptures left out to dry can be painted with acrylics (give them a white primer coat first).

25

Red Cabbage
CHEMISTRY SET

Use a natural pH indicator to test for acids.

If you want to score yourself a free chemistry set, hang around the kitchen the next time someone is cutting up a red cabbage. Those purple leaves do more than just add crunch to salads and coleslaw: they also contain pigments that change color in response to how acidic something is. When you chop the leaves and boil them, the purple juice left behind can instantly tell you if something is an acid or, the opposite, a base.

MATERIALS

- 2 quart-size mason jars (one of these should have measurement lines)
- Several half-pint mason jars
- 1 cup chopped red cabbage leaves
- Water
- Strainer
- Samples to test: Baking soda, egg white, lemon juice, vinegar, dish soap, cola, an antacid like Alka-Seltzer or Tums

SAFETY FIRST: This experiment involves using a microwave and should be done with adult supervision. Use potholders to handle hot jars.

INSTRUCTIONS

1 Put the chopped cabbage in one of the quart jars. It should fill it about halfway. Fill the jar to the quart line with water and microwave the jar on high for 5 minutes. Using potholders, set the hot jar where the cabbage mixture can steep and cool for 10 minutes.

2 Pour the juice into the other quart jar, using a strainer or the jar lid to hold back the chopped cabbage. It should be a rich purple color.

VINEGAR

COLA

LEMON JUICE

TELL ME MORE

One of the oldest tests for pH, dating back to around 1300, uses a dye called litmus, which is extracted from lichens (that grayish green stuff that grows on rocks and trees). The litmus is made into special paper that turns red or blue when it touches acids or bases. You can make your own litmus paper by soaking a coffee filter in cabbage juice, letting it dry, and then cutting it into strips for dipping into liquids.

3 Pour about 2 ounces of cabbage juice into each of the half-pint jars. These are your test samples. Set one jar aside to use for comparing colors later. An untouched sample like this is called a control.

4 Slowly add a test substance to each jar, 1 teaspoon at a time, and observe any changes.

What to Watch For

When acids (like vinegar and lemon juice) are added, the juice should turn a richer red than your control sample. Bases (like baking soda and egg white) turn it more purple or blue. Extremely base substances (such as ammonia) turn it yellow-green.

What's Going On

The red cabbage juice is a pH indicator. It gets its color from pigments called *anthocyanins*, which react when they come in contact with anything acidic or basic (anthocyanins are also in certain berries; see Very Berry Ink, page 79).

The pH (which stands for potential of hydrogen) of a substance is a measure of how acidic or basic it is. The most acidic substances have a pH of 0, while the most basic have a pH of 14. Pure water sits right in the middle, at 7. Many different kinds of scientists use pH in their work, from soil experts to oceanographers.

CONTROL

EGG WHITE

DISH SOAP

BAKING SODA

A PENNY
for Your Scientific Thoughts
Shine up old coins, then make them dull again.

Somewhere in your house there's probably a jar filled with grimy old pennies. In this experiment, you can transform those dull coins so they sparkle like they just came from the mint. Look for pennies dated 1982 or earlier, as they have more copper in them. Then, to demonstrate how pennies get that old look — and why the Statue of Liberty is green — you can make them grow old before your eyes.

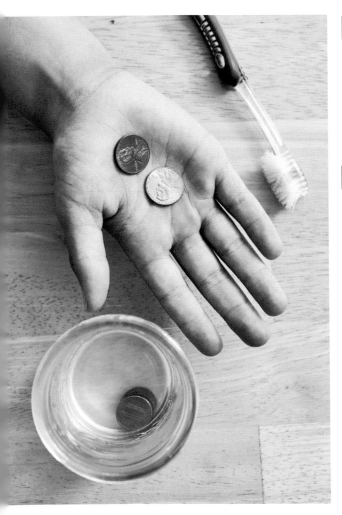

MATERIALS

2 pint-size (or smaller) mason jars, one with two-piece lid

White vinegar

Salt

Several dull pennies

Old toothbrush

Paper towels

INSTRUCTIONS

To SHINE

1 Mix ¼ cup white vinegar and 1 teaspoon salt in a jar, and stir to dissolve the salt. Add three or four pennies. Let the pennies soak for a few minutes. Do you notice any changes?

2 Scrub the pennies with an old toothbrush and some of the salt-vinegar solution, then rinse them in fresh water and dry them on a paper towel. How do they look now?

To AGE a penny

1 Place a folded paper towel in the bottom of another jar and wet it with the salt-vinegar solution. Dip the pennies in the solution and place them in the jar on the wet paper towel. Cover the jar with the lid to keep the towel moist.

2 Check the pennies after a few hours, then observe them over the next several days.

What to Watch For

By the second day, the pennies in the jar should have some blue-green blotches on their surface, a substance called malachite. After a few days, they should look old and cruddy again. But don't worry. Once you've seen enough, you can restore their shine with more vinegar and salt. Just remember to rinse the clean pennies with fresh water and dry them thoroughly.

What's Going On?

If you've ever left your bike out in the rain, you've encountered iron oxide, what most people call rust. Rust forms through oxidation, a chemical reaction that occurs when iron is exposed to oxygen and moisture. Copper pennies oxidize, too, and the result is a brownish coating of copper oxide.

In the first part of this experiment, the vinegar and salt dissolved the copper oxide on the penny, and the toothbrush restored the original copper shine. But it turns out that copper oxidizes another way if there is salt around, because salt (sodium chloride) contains chlorine. When copper is exposed to chlorine and oxygen, the result is that blue-green substance called malachite.

SCIENCE IN REAL LIFE

Perhaps the most famous example of oxidized copper is the Statue of Liberty. If you could find a big enough bathtub and enough vinegar, you could make her shine like a new penny. But sitting above the salty waters of New York Harbor, out in the wind and rain, she wouldn't stay shiny for long. In time, she'd have her familiar greenish blue coating again.

Fun with CRYSTALS

Grow glittering crystals from a saturated solution.

What do a big flashy diamond, a perfect snowflake, and a grain of sugar have in common? All three are examples of crystals, nature's most bedazzling creation. This experiment demonstrates how cooling and evaporation can force crystals out of a saturated solution. It takes some patience, but it's worth it. After all, you get to eat the results!

MATERIALS*

- Pint-size (or 12-ounce) mason jar
- 2 wooden skewers, sharp tips broken off
- Medium pot
- 1 cup water
- 3 cups white sugar
- Spoon or other stirrer
- Food coloring (optional)
- Spring clothespins

This formula makes two skewers. To make more, just increase the amounts of water and sugar.

SAFETY FIRST: This experiment requires using a hot stovetop. Be sure an adult is present.

TELL ME MORE

Crystallized sugar, or rock candy, has a long history, dating back more than a thousand years. It is believed to have originated in Iran, where the first candy makers grew their sugar crystals on twigs and colored them with natural dyes made from plants and insects.

INSTRUCTIONS

1 Heat the water in the pot until it starts to boil.

2 Slowly add the sugar to the boiling water, half a cup at a time, stirring between additions to dissolve the sugar. The syrup will be cloudy at first, but keep cooking and stirring until it turns clear. Once that happens, remove the pot from the heat and let the syrup cool for 15 to 20 minutes.

3 Prepare the skewers by soaking them in the hot syrup, then coating them with dry sugar and setting them on a plate to dry while the syrup cools. Using raw or turbinado sugar, which are both coarser than white sugar, may give a better result.

4 Carefully pour the cooled syrup into the jar, filling it at least halfway but leaving an inch or so at the top. Stir in several drops of food coloring, if you like.

5 Place the coated skewers in the jar, clipping them in place with a clothespin set across the mouth. The skewers should be about an inch from the bottom of the jar, and should not touch the sides.

6 Place the jars where they can sit undisturbed for at least a week.

What to Watch For

Crystals should begin to form on the skewers overnight, but it may take longer. Over the next few days, as the water in the solution evaporates, the crystals should continue to grow and solidify. If a crust forms on the surface of the syrup, carefully break it and remove the pieces. When the crystals are big enough, usually after a week or longer, remove the skewers and set them on a plate to dry.

What's Going On

Sucrose, or table sugar, is a crystal, which means its molecules fit together in an orderly pattern and it has a distinctive shape (grains of sugar, for example, are cubes with flat sides). Salt and diamonds are also crystals (for more, see String of Stalactites, page 46).

When you add sugar to water, the crystals dissolve to form a solution. Heating the solution lets you dissolve still more sugar, because hot water can hold more dissolved sugar than cold, but at a certain point the solution becomes saturated, meaning no more crystals will dissolve into it.

As the saturated solution cools and the water starts to evaporate over time, the crystals start to precipitate, or come out of the solution. They look for something to form onto (called a nucleation site), such as the sugar-coated skewer, and return to their original crystal shape.

GROW SOME ALUM ICE

For a close-up look at another crystal in action, give some rocks a coating of alum "ice." Used in pickling, among other things, alum (potassium aluminum sulfate) is a mineral that you can find in the supermarket spice section.

Start by arranging some clean rocks and pebbles at the bottom of a pint-size mason jar (preferably one with smooth sides for better viewing). In another pint-size mason jar, microwave ½ cup of water until it's boiling, about 2 minutes.

Using potholders, remove the hot jar and carefully add 2 ounces of alum, stirring until it dissolves. Pour the alum-water mixture over the rocks in the other jar and then let the jar sit uncovered and undisturbed.

Observe the jar over the next few hours. Soon the rocks will be covered with an ice-like coating of crystals.

SAFETY FIRST: This experiment requires using a microwave. Be sure an adult is present. Use potholders to handle hot jars.

SCIENCE IN REAL LIFE

Geodes, those crystal-filled rocks you often see in gift shops and museums, form through a similar process. Over thousands of years, water rich with minerals seeps into spaces in lava and other soft rocks, leaving behind layers of variously colored crystals.

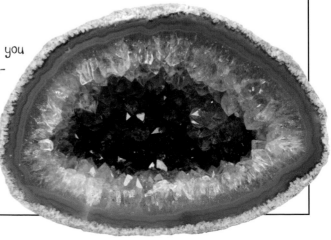

A BETTER BUBBLE

Experiment to create your own custom bubble mix.

Once upon a time, kids blew soap bubbles just for fun, and no one thought much about it. That was then. Now, adult "bubble masters" use secret soap mixes and custom wands to create monstrous bubbles as big as city buses. On stage, on television, and on YouTube, "bubble sculptors" create bubbles within bubbles, caterpillars made of bubbles, and even bubbles they can stand inside.

Soap bubbles have come a long way, and we have science to thank for it. By understanding the laws of chemistry and physics, today's bubble masters have taken their art to new heights. You can get in on the action yourself by blending your own custom bubble mixes. Then you can experiment to see which produces the biggest, strongest, and most colorful bubbles.

MATERIALS

3 quart-size mason jars with two-piece lids

Water

Dishwashing soap (preferably Dawn or Joy brands*)

Glycerin (sold at drugstores and craft stores**)

Guar gum ***

*Other brands might work, but bubble experts generally recommend these.

**Glycerin costs about $7 for 6 ounces at a drugstore, so some people use corn syrup instead.

***This food thickener is often sold in supermarkets (Bob's Red Mill is one brand). You need only a small amount, though, so check the bulk food section.

INSTRUCTIONS

Make the Basic Formula

3 cups water

2 tablespoons dishwashing soap

You can make bubbles with a mix of just dishwashing soap and water, but they won't be very big and they'll pop very quickly. That's why serious bubble makers add other ingredients to make their bubbles more stretchy and durable. Just a little bit of a key ingredient can make a huge difference in your bubbles! See for yourself by testing the different formulas. Label each formula so you can note its particular strengths and weaknesses.

Add GLYCERIN for Strength

3 cups water
2 tablespoons dishwashing soap
Glycerin

Also known as glycerol, glycerin is a humectant, a substance that keeps things moist. Bubbles burst when they dry out, so adding glycerin can make them last longer. Most formulas call for about 2 teaspoons per batch, but for extra strong bubbles, experiment with adding up to 4 tablespoons (2 ounces) per batch. The drawback: it makes your bubbles heavier and doesn't make them bigger.

Add GUAR GUM for Size

3 cups water
2 tablespoons dishwashing soap
Glycerin
Guar gum

For amazing monster-size bubbles, you need an extra stretchy formula. You can achieve that by adding a small amount of a polymer, such as guar gum, a food thickener. (For more about polymers, see What's Going On, page 21.)

To help the guar gum dissolve better, mix ¼ teaspoon of the powder with enough glycerin to create a paste. Mix the paste into the water, then add the dishwashing soap, and give everything a good stir.

Take It Further

Some bubble formulas call for baking soda, which is said to improve the performance and stability of larger bubbles. This acidic cooking powder changes the pH of the mix to make it more neutral. Add about ½ teaspoon per quart, first mixed into a paste with glycerin, as you did with the guar gum. Add this *after* adding the guar gum, water, and dish soap, then cap the jar and turn it over to blend everything together. Can you observe any difference in your bubbles?

CONTINUED →

What to Watch For

See how long the bubbles last, how strong they are, how high they fly, even how colorful they are. Try them indoors and outdoors, on a calm day and a windy day. See how each formula works when you use a big wand or a small blower (see Homemade Bubble Wands, opposite). The brand of dishwashing soap you use can have a big impact on your final mix. Dawn and Joy are recommended, so if your bubbles are not performing well, try one of those.

For more tips and expert advice, check out Soap Bubble Wiki online, where you can read reviews of mixtures, see amazing photos, and learn more about the role of various ingredients.

What's Going On

A bubble is a ball of air surrounded by a thin film of liquid. Water alone is not stretchy enough to hold the air, but a mix with dishwashing soap is elastic, like a balloon. Bubbles pop when the water on their surface evaporates or touches anything dry. Adding a humectant, such as glycerin, to your mix slows down evaporation, making the bubbles last longer. Adding a polymer, such as guar gum, makes the bubbles far more elastic so they can stretch to huge sizes.

TELL ME MORE

Since bubbles pop from evaporation, the best time to blow them outdoors is when the air is calm and muggy, such as after a rain shower. On colder days, however, your bubbles may fly higher, because your warm breath is lighter than the cold air. In extremely cold weather, you can watch your bubbles freeze into ice orbs (or watch it on YouTube). And if you really want your bubbles to last, keep them in a sealed jar with a little bubble solution on the bottom. Famous bubble entertainer Eiffel Plasterer (Google him!) is said to have kept a bubble this way for nearly a year!

HOMEMADE BUBBLE WANDS

Sure, you could use those plastic rings that come in store-bought bubble mixes. But other options are all around you. Try using one of these.

A string wand. These devices use a circle of string wick to make immense bubbles. For a simple homemade version, thread about 3 feet of string or yarn through two straws and tie it in a knot. Holding a straw in each hand, dip the device in a wide flat container of mix (see top photo, page 35). You can find instructions for other wands online at Soap Bubble Wiki.

The metal ring from a mason jar. Add a clothespin for a handle and pour your bubble mix into a shallow plate for dipping.

A pipe cleaner. Bend it into a lollipop shape. The fuzz holds the soap mix like a paintbrush.

A wire coat hanger. Bend it into a large lollipop shape. Use a plate, Frisbee, or any other wide and flat container to hold your mix. For monster bubbles, wrap the wire hoop in a cotton shoelace to hold even more liquid. Tape the handle for a grip.

EARTH SCIENCE
for Earthlings

Not so long ago, people looked around and thought for sure the Earth was flat. Others felt the ground shake and thought angry gods or giant creatures were to blame. We know a lot more now, but we still have many questions about the world in which we live. Earth science tries to answer them. How did our planet form? What is it made of? How are humans changing it?

Earth scientists help us deal with threats like climate change, earthquakes, soil erosion, and water pollution. Their work helps us understand why life started here millions of years ago, and what it will need in the future. Want to explore the mysteries of our amazing planet? Start by thinking about the fascinating clues it has left for us — towering mountains, spectacular canyons, sandy beaches. For an earth scientist, there really is no place like home.

JAR-RARIUM

Create a thriving miniature landscape.

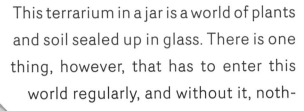

This terrarium in a jar is a world of plants and soil sealed up in glass. There is one thing, however, that has to enter this world regularly, and without it, nothing would live: light. Fortunately, the clear glass lets the sunshine in, and from that, the plants can make the food they need to survive. Keep your "jar-rarium" near a window where it gets just enough light (but not too much), and it can last for years.

soil

filter

charcoal

pebbles

MATERIALS

Wide-mouth quart-size (or larger) mason jar with two-piece lid

Pebbles

Large spoon

Activated charcoal (sold at pet stores; See Tell Me More, opposite page)

Coffee filter

Scissors

Potting mix

Spray mister filled with water

Paper towel

Moss and other low-growing woodland plants that will fit in the jar

Stones and other decorations

Fork or other long-handled tool

INSTRUCTIONS

1 Before you go out to gather plants, collect all the other materials you'll need and put them in your workspace.

2 Collect your plants. Look for moss and other low-growing plants that will fit in the jar (see Collecting Notes, at right). If you prefer to buy plants, ask at your local garden center or nursery for varieties that won't outgrow your terrarium. There are many to choose from!

3 Cover the bottom of the jar with an inch or so of pebbles. This creates an area where excess water can drain.

4 Spoon a half-inch layer of activated charcoal on top of the pebbles.

5 Using the jar lid as a template, cut a circle from the coffee filter that is a little smaller than the diameter of the jar. Lay it over the charcoal. This prevents soil from mixing with the pebbles and charcoal, keeping the drainage area clear.

6 Carefully spoon in about 2 inches of potting mix, or enough to fill the jar one-third of the way. Mist the soil with the sprayer until thoroughly dampened, but not soggy.

CONTINUED →

COLLECTING NOTES

Wild plants that grow well in terrariums are usually found in shaded, wooded areas with moist soil. Look for mosses, small ferns, and low-growing ground covers like violets (but watch out for poison ivy!). Only dig where you have permission.

Using a garden trowel or a large spoon, dig around the plant's roots, keeping as much soil attached as you can. Put the plants in a small plastic bag or tub and keep the roots damp and protected from sunlight until you get home.

TELL ME MORE

Charcoal is one of the oldest water-purifying materials, dating back to ancient Egypt. Activated charcoal works like a sponge, trapping impurities and other waste materials in its many tiny holes. If you have a fish tank, you might have used it in your aquarium filter. You don't have to use it in the jar-rarium, but without it, the inside might begin to smell a bit swampy after a while!

7 If needed, lightly trim the roots and branches so the plants fit in the jar. Working with a fork or other long-handled tool, dig into the soil and press the moss and plants into place. Add any other decorations.

8 Mist the plants lightly, taking care to moisten the soil near the plants' roots (without flooding them out!). Use a paper towel to carefully wipe the inside walls of the jar. Screw on the two-piece cap and place the jar in a bright place, but not directly in the sun.

What to Watch For

Observe the jar-rarium closely over the next few days. If the sides get cloudy or completely covered with water drops, take off the cap for an hour or so to let the water evaporate (a little water on the sides is normal). If the soil starts to look dry, give it a little more misting. If plants turn yellow or otherwise look unhappy, or start to die, cut them out and consider replacing them.

What's Going On

A jar-rarium is what scientists call an ecosystem. Just like on earth, the plants, soil, and water all work in harmony, allowing the system to thrive. The plants draw water up through their roots, then release it through pores (tiny holes) in their leaves, a process called transpiration (see Speak like a Scientist, page 67). The water then collects on the sides of the jar and falls back on the soil, to be reused by the plant.

When plants create food through the process of photosynthesis, they give off oxygen. The oxygen is then used by bacteria in the soil, which break down old plant material such as leaves and give off carbon dioxide. The plants then use the carbon dioxide again, in a repeating cycle that keeps all these living things happy.

SCIENCE IN REAL LIFE

Imagine a jar-rarium big enough for people to live in! Such a place does exist, and if you are near Oracle, Arizona, you can go for a tour. Called Biosphere 2, this complex of huge greenhouses covers more than three acres. Inside the glass walls are an entire rainforest, a desert, farms, and even a small ocean with a coral reef. People have lived sealed inside it for years at a time.

AT-HOME MUSEUM

Display your finds from the natural world.

Curious scientists are always gathering interesting specimens: unusual rocks, say, or dead beetles, or even the ghostlike skin of a snake. Who could pass up these gifts from the natural world? (Not us.) Such treasures deserve to be properly organized and displayed, both to protect them from damage and to allow others to appreciate them.

MATERIALS

A number of mason jars in various sizes and shapes, preferably with smooth sides, and lids

Index cards or other labels

Various specimens (here are just some of the options):
- Rocks
- Beach sand
- Shells
- Sea glass
- Seedpods
- Pinecones
- Acorns
- Tree bark
- Dead insects
- Feathers
- Bones

Magnifying glass

INSTRUCTIONS

1 Place each specimen in an appropriately sized jar. For instance, put tiny stones into a small jam jar. Or large shells into a quart jar.

2 Label each specimen with its name, where you collected it, and the date you found it. For a more official look, create the labels on your computer.

3 Organize your collection the way a scientist would, grouping things by categories that make sense or that tell a story. You might have beach sand from family trips, organized by when or where you collected it. Or you might group your specimens under bigger categories, such as Animals, Plants, or Minerals.

CONTINUED →

4 Set up your collection where it can be easily seen and examined, such as on its own set of shelves. Keep a magnifying glass handy so visitors can get a closer look at the specimens, and set out various reference books for identifying natural objects.

5 Create a quiz for visitors to your museum. Place an unusual specimen in a Mystery Jar and ask a question on an accompanying label. Can you identify this? Where did it come from?

Take It Further

To broaden the variety of your collection, ask friends and relatives in distant states or other countries to send contributions to your museum. Ask them for natural history specimens that are unique to their area, or that have a personal significance to them. Be sure to label these, and note the donor's name!

TELL ME MORE

Scientists are not generally known for joking around, but when they have the chance to name a new species of plant or animal, they sometimes can't help themselves. Just take a look at these unusual scientific names.

Gelae baen
A small, oval beetle that looks like a Jelly Bean (get it?). Its relatives: *Gelae rol*, *Gelae fish*, *Gelae belae*, and *Gelae donut*.

Spongiforma squarepantsii
A species of mushroom, found in Malaysia in 2010, whose spongy appearance inspired researchers to name it after the cartoon character.

Agra cadabra
One member of a punnily named family of Amazonian beetles that also includes *Agra vation* and *Agra phobia*.

Scaptoa Beyonceae
A rare species of horse fly with a curvaceous abdomen and golden hairs, named in honor of Beyonce in 2011.

SPEAK like a SCIENTIST

You may have noticed that plants and animals on display at museums will often have a label that identifies them by a long name in another language. This is the scientific or Latin name, which tells scientists what family a plant or animal is part of, and something distinct about it. The name for human beings, for example, is *Homo sapiens*, which means "wise man." Carl Linnaeus, a Swedish botanist, zoologist, and physician, developed this two-part system for naming things, called binomial nomenclature, in the 1700s. It is now used by museums and scientists around the world.

CATEGORIZING A CRICKET

Scientists classify animals and plants by analyzing what they have in common and then grouping them in categories with other organisms that are similar, a field of study called taxonomy. The field cricket (*Gryllus assimilis*), for example, is part of the broader cricket family (Grillidae). The family is part of the broader Orthoptera order (which includes grasshoppers and locust), which is part of the broader class of insects, and so on. For more about scientific names, see Speak like a Scientist, opposite page.

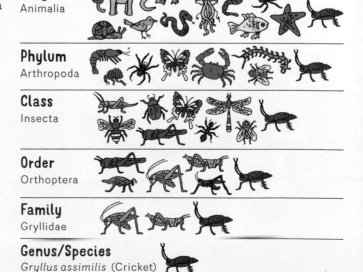

Kingdom
Animalia

Phylum
Arthropoda

Class
Insecta

Order
Orthoptera

Family
Gryllidae

Genus/Species
Gryllus assimilis (Cricket)

String of STALACTITES

Grow some underground décor for your kid cave.

You think growing bigger takes a long time? Try being a stalactite. Those drippy columns you see in caves grow just a few inches every thousand years! You can observe how they do it by growing your very own string of stalactite crystals. The best part is, it won't take a thousand years! (More like a week.) Set up your experiment where no one will touch it, check your drip bowl every day, and watch what happens.

MATERIALS

2 pint-size mason jars

Piece of yarn, about 4 feet long

Scissors

2 bendy straws

Skewer or pipe cleaner

Hot tap water

Baking soda, about ½ cup

Spoon or other stirrer

Food coloring (optional)

Bowl for drips

SPEAK like a SCIENTIST

Here's a handy way to tell your stalactites from your stalagmites: stala**C**tites hang down from the **C**-ling while stala**G**mites rise up from the **G**-round.

INSTRUCTIONS

1 Fold the yarn in half and twist it together to make a thick strand. Cut the bendable "elbows" from the straws, leaving about an inch of the straight part on each end. Thread the straws on the yarn, using a skewer or pipe cleaner to push the yarn through.

2 Fill the jars about two-thirds full with hot tap water. Spoon in baking soda, a tablespoon at a time, to each jar and stir to dissolve it. Keep adding baking soda and stirring until the powder no longer dissolves and instead starts to gather on the bottom of the jar (it should take 3 to 5 tablespoons for each jar). You've created a saturated solution (see Fun with Crystals, page 30). Add a few drops of food coloring if you want.

3 Set up the jars up as shown, with the drip bowl between them. Remember: the crystals are very delicate and will fall easily if jostled, so set up your experiment in a place where you can leave it for several days.

Straw elbows hold the yarn in place.

4 Soak the yarn in the solution, making sure it's wet all the way through the straws. Hang it between the jars using the elbows to hold it in place as shown. The ends of the yarn must be in the solution and the center of the yarn must be lower than the level of the solution in the jars, forming a drip point.

What to Watch For

The solution should start dripping into the bowl right away. You'll begin to see crystals form after a day or so. Over the next few days, observe how much they grow. When the bowl gets full, carefully pour the solution back into the jars.

What's Going On

Baking soda, or sodium bicarbonate, is a crystal, meaning it forms in a distinctive shape. As the solution of dissolved baking soda moves through the yarn, thanks to capillary action (see Walking Watercolors, page 108), the water evaporates, forcing the baking soda to form again as a solid, a process called crystallization.

SCIENCE IN REAL LIFE

Real stalactites are created through a similar process. In certain caves, water flows through soft rock, such as limestone, and carries away dissolved minerals. As the mineralized water drips from the ceiling it creates an icicle-like column of minerals and crystals. The world's largest stalactite is more than 25 feet long!

CORNSTARCH QUICKSAND

Make a solid liquid. Or is it a liquid solid?

Experts will tell you that if you ever happen to be trapped in quicksand, you shouldn't panic and thrash about, which will only sink you deeper. Instead, you should lie back so you float on the watery sand, then slowly — *slowly!* — paddle your way to solid ground. So now you know what to do if you happen to fall into a huge vat of this cornstarch and water mixture. Like quicksand, it's a mysterious ooze, somewhere between a liquid and a solid, and it's full of surprises.

MATERIALS

Any size mason jar with two-piece lid

Water

Cornstarch

Wooden spoon or other stirrer

Shallow pan

INSTRUCTIONS

1 Using a formula of one part water to two parts cornstarch, mix up however much quicksand you want. (For a large batch, use one cup of water and two cups of cornstarch in a quart jar.) Use a stiff wooden spoon to stir the mixture. It will be hard to mix together, but keep at it! Eventually, it will form a thick paste.

What's Going On

You've created a colloidal solution, a mixture made up of very tiny particles suspended in water. Quicksand, which is just sand suspended in water, is very similar. These types of mixtures can act like both solids and liquids, depending on what you are doing to them.

The eighteenth-century scientist Sir Isaac Newton (of "law of gravity" fame) studied fluids and came up with rules for how the ideal ones should act. Colloidal solutions are so weird, they are referred to as non-Newtonian fluids.

2 Pour the quicksand into a shallow pan and walk your fingers across it. When they sink in, try to pull them out fast, like a panicked person might, and see what happens. Lift some mixture in your hands and squeeze it. Release your grip and see what happens.

NOTE: Your quicksand will last a while stored in the jar, but when you want to get rid of it, don't pour it down the drain (it can cause a clog). Instead, throw it away or compost it.

What to Watch For

The mixture will feel stiff if you stir quickly, but more loose if you stir slowly. Tap your stirrer on the mixture's surface. It feels solid. Scoop the mixture up with the stirrer. It flows off like a liquid!

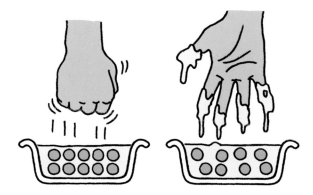

Under pressure, a non-Newtonian fluid acts like a solid. When not under pressure, it acts like a liquid.

TELL ME MORE

In 2008, science educator and author Steve Spangler went on *The Ellen DeGeneres Show* to demonstrate that you could actually walk across a vat of cornstarch quicksand, as long as you did it quickly. He had a cement truck mix 2,500 pounds of cornstarch and 250 gallons of water, which filled a 7-foot-long tub with ooze. Then he invited an audience member up to give it a try. She hopped right across.

HOMEMADE COMPASS

Discover the power of Earth's magnetic fields.

Magnets can do so many amazing things — make high-speed trains hover off the ground, allow a junkyard crane to lift and move cars, and even let doctors peer inside your body through magnetic resonance imaging (MRI) scans. But perhaps the most amazing magnet is one we rarely notice: the Earth's own magnetic field. Caused by hot metal moving inside our planet, this web of invisible energy is what keeps a compass needle pointing north, which in turn has allowed humans to find their way around the planet for the last thousand or so years. See how it works with this simple experiment.

MATERIALS

Wide-mouth pint-size (or smaller) mason jar

A strong magnet (not the flat flexible kind)

Standard sewing needle

Wax paper

Scissors

Water

INSTRUCTIONS

1 To magnetize the sewing needle, hold the eye in your fingertips, press the magnet flat against the needle, and rub toward the point. Do this about 50 times, stroking lightly and always in one direction. (Note: the magnetism will fade with time, so repeat the process when your compass stops working.)

SPEAK like a SCIENTIST

Numerous animals are able to detect the earth's magnetic field and use it to navigate, a sense called magnetoreception. The growing list of creatures that scientists believe have this gift includes homing pigeons and other birds, bats, bees, sea turtles, and even fruit flies, but, sadly, not humans.

2 From the wax paper, cut a circle with a diameter roughly the length of your needle. Carefully push the needle through the wax paper in two places so it is secured evenly across the center of the circle. Fill the jar with water and float the needle in the center.

What to Watch For

The floating needle should spin until it is pointing north and south. (Check the reading with an actual compass or the digital compass on a smart phone.) If the wax paper moves toward the jar's sides, push it back to the center. Make sure there are no magnets near the jar!

What's Going On

The magnetized needle, like the needle of an actual compass, moves in response to the Earth's magnetic field. The wax paper raft allows the needle to turn easily, so even the very weak field that surrounds the planet can make it move. To see how sensitive it is, place your magnet near the jar. What happens to the needle?

TELL ME MORE

The earth's magnetic field has not always been the way it is now, with the magnetic north pole located off Ellesmere Island in northern Canada, near the earth's actual, or geographic, north pole. Scientists have discovered that the magnetic north pole is moving, traveling around 35 miles each year.

Even more dramatic, from time to time, the magnetic poles unpredictably flip, meaning all compass needles would point south. Scientists know this by studying old rocks and lava. When lava cools, the iron in it aligns with the magnetic field at that time. From this, they can tell that the poles have reversed over the eons.

And get this: the pattern suggests that the earth may be overdue for the poles to shift again!

DEAD SEA IN A JAR

Learn why it's easier to float in the ocean.

The Dead Sea, a salt lake in the desert in the Middle East, has water that's nearly 10 times saltier than the ocean. For thousands of years, visitors have marveled at how easily they can float on its surface. Plants and fish, however, can't live in the water, which explains its creepy name. How does salt make things float? In this experiment, you'll discover the Dead Sea's secret and then visit the north and south poles to learn how melting ice mixes with salt water.

MATERIALS

- 2 wide-mouth pint-size mason jars
- Warm tap water
- Salt
- 2 raw eggs
- Spoon

INSTRUCTIONS

1 Add 1 cup of warm tap water to each of the jars, using the markings on the side.

2 Add 3 tablespoons of salt to one jar, and stir to dissolve it.

3 Place an egg in the fresh water jar. What happens?

4 Now place the other egg in the salt water jar. What happens?

SPEAK like a SCIENTIST

When scientists want to say that something is capable of floating, they say it is buoyant. The word is related to buoy, those floating markers used to guide boats.

What to Watch For

The egg should sink in the fresh water but float in the salt water. With the egg floating in the salt water, add more fresh water. The egg should start to sink. Add just the right amount, and the egg will hover in the middle of the jar, not sinking but not floating, either.

What's Going On

Things sink or float depending on whether they are more or less dense than the liquid they are in (for more, see Tower of Liquids, page 110). Density is how heavy something is for its size. The egg is more dense than fresh water, but less dense than salt water.

Adding salt to the water makes the water more dense, so it supports objects that might sink in fresh water. Adding fresh water to the salt water makes it less dense, so objects start to sink.

TAKE IT FURTHER

Use the jars of fresh water and salt water for another experiment, one that demonstrates how cold and salt affect the flow of water in the oceans. Make ice cubes from colored water and place one in each jar. Watch what happens to the colored water as the cubes melt.

In the fresh water, the cold melt water sinks, mixing with the water in the jar. In the other jar, however, the dense salt water holds the cold fresh water in a layer on top. Similar forces are at work in the oceans, especially near the Earth's two poles.

53

How's the wEATHER?

METEOROLOGY PROJECTS FOR A RAINY (OR SUNNY OR CLOUDY) DAY

It's no surprise that people love talking about the weather. It affects us all, so almost everybody has something to say about it. But it's also a topic with a serious side, which is why there's a whole field of science dedicated to understanding it. The study of weather, or meteorology, allows us to better understand and predict the many forms of dangerous weather: hurricanes, tornados, blizzards, droughts, heat waves, and the like.

By measuring and recording the weather, scientists also can see patterns and offer important predictions about climate change, another issue that affects us all. Weather is as big and complicated as the Earth itself, but with the right instruments and experiments, you can see and understand the forces at work, right in your own home. The following projects let you do just that.

BALLOON BAROMETER

Here's a fact that might make your eyes bug out: the weight of all the air that's stacked above you puts 14.7 pounds of pressure on every square inch of your body. We don't notice this air pressure except when we travel to higher places where the pressure is lower — when we ride in elevators, say, or fly in airplanes, and feel the change in our ears.

A barometer is an instrument that precisely measures air pressure. By looking at whether it's low or high, or rising or falling, meteorologists can tell what type of weather is on the way. Here's how you can make your own and use it to become your family's meteorologist.

MATERIALS

- 2 quart-size mason jars, one wide-mouth
- 12-inch balloon
- Thick rubber band
- 2 straws, bendy parts trimmed off
- Scissors
- Glue
- Tape
- Cardboard or stiff paper
- Barometric Pressure Chart (page 129)

CONTINUED →

INSTRUCTIONS

1 Blow up the balloon to stretch it, then let out the air and cut off the neck. Stretch the balloon tight over the mouth of the jar, pulling it over the ridges where the cap screws on. Place a thick rubber band (like the ones that come on broccoli) around the edge to hold it in place.

2 Join two straws together by squeezing the end of one and sticking it into the end of the other. Cut a slit in one end of this new long double straw and insert a pointer arrow cut from the cardboard or stiff paper.

3 Squeeze a line of glue from the center of the balloon to the edge of the jar. Set the non-pointer end of the straw in the glue, support the other end with another jar, and gently tape the straw in place until the glue dries (with white glue, this may take overnight).

4 While the glue dries, make your barometric pressure chart. You can design your own or use the one on page 129. Glue the chart to a sheet of cardboard or stiff paper, and tape it to the other jar so it stands upright.

5 Once the glue is thoroughly dry, place your barometer where it won't be disturbed, out of direct sunlight, in a spot where the temperature remains constant, such as a basement. Set up the chart next to it, and mark where the arrow is pointing.

What to Watch For

Check the barometer daily and mark where the arrow is pointing, noting the date and time. Check your barometer's readings against the actual air pressure, also called the barometric pressure, which you can find online (at weather.gov or a similar site). Write that number where the arrow is pointing. If you do this for a few days, you'll have a chart that shows the range of barometric pressure in your area.

What's Going On

High air pressure forces the balloon to sag down into the jar, which makes the arrow point higher. Low air pressure allows the balloon to curve up, causing the arrow to point lower. Rising and falling temperatures will also cause the balloon to change shape, so be sure to place your barometer where the temperature is constant.

SCIENCE IN REAL LIFE

The invention of the barometer is credited to Evangelista Torricelli, an Italian physicist and friend of Galileo Galilei (of telescope fame). Torricelli built his version in Florence in 1643, and while it sounds like a type of pasta, Torricelli's Tube was actually a glass pipe filled with mercury — definitely not edible!

Other designs also feature liquid in glass containers, such as the so-called "weatherglass," whose thin arm holds liquid that rises and falls as the air pressure changes.

TAKE IT FURTHER

Your barometer can help you predict changes in the weather. During the course of a day, observe which way the arrow is moving. When the air pressure is rising, the weather should be fair. When the pressure is dropping, unsettled weather could be on the way. Compare your readings to the actual weather and see if your forecasts are correct!

TINY TORNADO

Tornados are one of Earth's most powerful weather events, causing dozens of deaths and hundreds of injuries each year in the United States alone. Scientists continue to study how they form, hoping someday to be able to better predict where they will strike next. In this experiment, you can re-create the distinctive funnel cloud of a tornado in a jar and observe its remarkable spinning motion — from the safety of your own home!

MATERIALS

Quart-size mason jar, preferably with smooth sides, with two-piece lid

Water

Food coloring

Dishwashing soap

Glitter or seed beads (optional)

Vinegar (if needed)

INSTRUCTIONS

1 Fill the jar with water, leaving an inch or so of space at the top.

2 Add about a teaspoon of dishwashing soap and a couple of drops of food coloring. To witness the effect of debris being swirled around by your tornado, add a sprinkle of glitter or some small beads.

3 Screw on the lid, check for leaks, and give everything a shake to mix it all up.

4 Set the soapy water spinning by moving the jar in a circular swirling motion for 5 to 10 seconds. Stop swirling, hold the jar up to a light or window, and witness the awesome power of nature.

What's Going On

When you swirl the jar, the fluid that's pressing against the sides of the jar spins faster than the fluid in the center. When you stop, the inner fluid keeps spinning while the portion against the sides starts to slow. Meanwhile, gravity is pulling everything down. The result is a spinning spiral called a vortex, the same shape you see when water drains out of a bathtub, in the circular winds of hurricanes, and in spiral galaxies like the Milky Way.

In a tornado, the vortex is set in motion by winds blowing in opposite directions. Powerful updrafts of warm air then lift the rolling air into a vertical spinning column that — if the conditions are right — leads to a tornado.

What to Watch For

When you stop swirling the jar, the soapy water continues to spin, creating a whirlpool that resembles the funnel cloud of a tornado, sweeping up anything in its path (as shown by the spinning glitter or beads). If your dishwashing soap creates too many bubbles, scoop them out and add a teaspoon or so of vinegar.

TELL ME MORE

In a typical year, some 1,000 tornados strike the United States, according to the National Oceanic and Atmospheric Administration. The strongest of these have winds in excess of 250 miles per hour. They can be as large as a mile wide and cause destruction for more than 50 miles!

CONJURE A CLOUD

Clouds may look pure and white, but they are actually built on dirt — or, more precisely, tiny specks of dust, soot, and smoke. The dust gives water in the air, known as water vapor, something to condense on, the same way a cool bathroom mirror offers the steam from a shower a place to collect. In the case of a cloud, the condensation is triggered when water vapor rises into the atmosphere and cools in the lower air pressure.

In this activity, we trigger the condensation with cooled air. It's the same process that creates fog, which is essentially a cloud that forms near the ground, when warm moist air meets cold.

MATERIALS

Quart-size mason jar

A plastic cup that sits in the jar with most of the cup below the rim

Ice cubes and cold water

Hot tap water

Matches

SAFETY FIRST: This experiment involves lighting matches and should be done with adult supervision.

INSTRUCTIONS

1 Fill the cup with ice cubes and add cold water.

2 Fill the jar with hot tap water, swirl it around, and pour it out, repeating a couple of times to warm up the jar. Add 2 or 3 inches of hot water to the jar and place it on the counter.

3 Drop a lit match into the water and immediately set the cup of ice water over the mouth. As you watch, wisps of cloud should begin forming.

What's Going On

Adding and swirling the hot water creates water vapor in the jar. Smoke particles from the lit match provide a collecting surface, and the ice water provides the cold that causes condensation. The result: your own cloud, captured in a jar. To set your cloud free, remove the cup.

Take It Further

You can also a capture a cloud in a jar using air pressure, but you'll have to pay close attention, as the results are subtle. When warm moist air rises in the atmosphere, its pressure and temperature drop. The air then expands and cools, triggering condensation. To reproduce this in a quart jar, first screw on a Jar Spout (see page 105).

Swirl in some hot water, pour out all but a little, then drop in a lit match. Take a breath, seal the spout with your lips (like you are playing a tuba), and blow into the jar to increase the air pressure. Suddenly stop blowing and look closely: can you see a thin mist of cloud inside?

Blow again, then release. As soon as you add pressure, the mist should vanish. When you stop, the air pressure drops and the cloud should appear. (It can help to shine a flashlight at the jar or hold it up to a light.) Unscrew the lid and you might see wisps of cloud float out.

TELL ME MORE

Contrails, those white lines high in the sky caused by passing jets, form because jet exhaust provides soot for water vapor to condense on, just like the match smoke does here. You can remember what causes them by thinking about their name: *contrail* is short for "condensation trail."

RAIN GAUGE

Gardeners know that keeping track of the rain is a sure way to keep your plants happy, because unlike us, they can't just run to the kitchen sink for a drink. The rule of thumb is that vegetables need about an inch of rain every week. But what is an inch of rain? How do you even measure that? This simple instrument will let you know.

MATERIALS

Straight-sided, wide-mouth quart-size mason jar with measurement lines, with two-piece lid

1-liter plastic bottle

Marker

Scissors

INSTRUCTIONS

1 To make the funnel for your gauge, insert the top of the plastic bottle into the mouth of the jar. Draw a line around bottle just above the rim of the jar. Cut all the way around the line and discard or recycle the bottom of the bottle.

2 Set the funnel in the jar so it's resting inside the mouth. Its top edge will sit just a bit over the rim. Screw on the jar's ring so the edge of the ring holds the funnel in place.

3 Set the jar outdoors in an open area, away from any overhanging buildings or trees that might interfere with rainfall. Ideally, the location will also be protected from high winds.

What to Watch For

After a rainstorm, check your gauge to see how much precipitation fell. A heavy rainstorm can result in as much as an inch of rain, but most showers produce a fraction of an inch. You can use the jar's measuring lines to estimate the amount of rainfall, but to get the exact measurement, remove the funnel and measure the depth of water in the jar with a ruler. Reset the gauge by pouring out the water.

What's Going On

Rainfall is measured in inches, so you need a device that can evenly gather and hold a sample of liquid, and that allows you to easily measure it. Any straight-sided cylinder will work, but a glass container with measuring lines allows you to see the level at a glance. The funnel slows down the evaporation of water from the jar, preserving the rain sample for longer. Since the funnel is the same diameter as the jar, it does not affect the gauge's accuracy.

TELL ME MORE

A quart-size rain gauge would have been no use on June 22, 1947, in the town of Holt, Missouri. On that day the town received a record-setting 12 inches of rain in just 42 minutes!

The Root of All Fun BOTANY

How important is botany, the science of plants? Well, without it, humans would not have been able to create our modern civilization because we'd have been too busy trying to find food every day. The science of botany and the development of agriculture gave us a reliable food supply, which in turn gave us time to pursue bigger things: exploring new frontiers, building cities where people could trade goods and share ideas, and developing schools and universities.

Today, plant scientists continue to make important discoveries, breeding new crops that taste better, provide more nutrition, resist diseases, and grow in harsh conditions. But working with plants is rewarding in other ways as well. It lets us help transform a small seed into a delicious head of broccoli, a spectacular sunflower, or an oak tree that offers shade on a hot day. So let's get growing!

CAPILLARY COLORS

Use colored water to give vegetables a new look.

Thirsty plants use their roots and stems like straws, sucking up water and nutrients to supply their sugar-producing leaves. This experiment lets you see just how they do it. The colored water travels up the plant and ends up in the leaves. The colors show up best in white-stalked Chinese or napa cabbage, but you can also use celery stalks with the leaves attached.

MATERIALS

Several pint-size (or quart-size) mason jars

Chinese cabbage or leafy celery*

Kitchen scissors

Water

Food coloring

Use slightly wilted leaves for best results.

INSTRUCTIONS

1 Break off several cabbage leaves or celery stalks. Even out the bottom edge with the scissors.

2 Add about 2 inches of water to each jar and stir in 20 or so drops of food coloring.

3 Place the leaves upright in the jars and set them in a place where you can observe them for a few days.

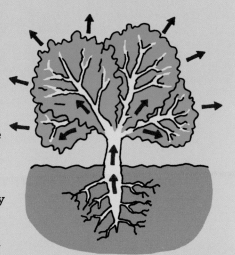

SPEAK like a SCIENTIST

The process by which plants move water from their roots to their leaves and then release it into the air is called transpiration. It's sort of like human perspiration, except you rarely see a plant sweat. After delivering important nutrients to the plant, the water is released through tiny holes (called stomata) on the undersides of the leaves.

How much water plants transpire depends on many things, such as the weather and the soil, but they can put out an amazing amount. Just one acre of corn can release more than 3,000 gallons a day. A large oak tree can give off 40,000 gallons of water in a year!

What to Watch For

During the next few hours or overnight (depending on how thirsty your cabbage is), you should see colors begin to appear on the white stem and on the edges of the leaves, then continue to spread throughout the leaf. The longer you let the leaves soak up the liquid, the darker the color should become.

What's Going On

As the leaf of a plant starts to dry out, it draws up water through tiny tubes in its stems called xylem. It does this using capillary action, the same process that lets a paper towel absorb a spill on your kitchen counter. (For more on this, see Walking Watercolors, page 108.) In a living plant, the xylem would get water from the roots. Here, the roots have been removed, so the xylem draw up the colored water right from the jar.

Take It Further

Give flowers with white blooms, such as carnations, some bold color using the same process. Cut the stems about 6 inches below the bloom and place them in jars with colored water. For a wild two-colored look, carefully split the stem with scissors, and place each half in a different color of water.

ROOT VIEW

Get a worm's-eye view of how roots grow.

Gardeners get a kick out of seeing their seedlings pop up each spring. But before those little green shoots can make their appearance, the seeds have to do something even more amazing. Buried in the ground, out of sight, they come to life through the process known as germination. Put some seeds in a mason jar filled with moist paper towels, and you can see it all unfold before your eyes.

MATERIALS

- Quart-size mason jar with two-piece lid
- Paper towels
- Colored paper napkins (optional)
- Craft stick or similar tool
- Large seeds (such as beans, peas, pumpkin, or squash)
- Water

SPEAK
like a
SCIENTIST

A plant's ability to send its roots down and its shoots up is called geotropism or gravitropism. Plants sense the pull of gravity and use that to steer their roots into the earth, where they can find water, and to send their shoots up into the air, where they can find light. Charles Darwin, best known for his theory of evolution, was one of the first scientists to document this ability. More recently, space scientists have found that plants trying to grow roots in space get confused without gravity to guide them.

1 Line the jar with paper towels or colored paper napkins. (The colored napkins are not necessary, but they provide a darker background for viewing the roots.) Ball up a dozen or so paper towels and stuff them into the middle of the jar.

2 Add enough water to soak the paper towels. They should be evenly moist, with a small puddle of water at the bottom of the jar.

3 Using a craft stick as a tool, tuck seeds between the outer layer of paper and the side of the jar, about halfway up, one on each side. The pressure from the wadded-up paper towels should hold the seeds in place.

4 Cover the jar with the lid and place it in a warm spot, out of direct sunlight. Observe it for the next few days, rolling the jar on its side from time to time to moisten the seeds and adding water if the towels dry out.

What to Watch For

Within a few days to a week, you should begin to see roots emerging from the seeds. Notice which direction the roots grow. Soon after, a green shoot should emerge. Move the jar to a sunny windowsill and remove the cap. Check the seeds every day and keep the towels moist. If all goes well, the seedlings might eventually grow right out of the jar!

If any of your seeds do not grow, they may be old and no longer viable (able to grow). Try some other seeds.

What's Going On

Germination is a reaction triggered by water and temperature. The water activates chemicals in the seed that start the process. First, the seed sends out a root, which grows downward seeking more water.

Next comes a shoot, growing upward, with green leaves that can transform the energy of the sun into food. Until it can sprout, the seed lives off its own supply of food. (For more, see Seedling Superman!, page 82.)

THE KITCHEN JAR-DEN

TURN VEGGIE LEFTOVERS INTO AN INDOOR GARDEN.

Plants usually start out as seeds, but that's not the only way you can grow them. You can sprout carrot fronds from leftover carrot tops and persuade a sweet potato to produce a spectacular ivy-like vine. Want to produce something even more impressive? Grow an avocado tree from a pit that you would otherwise throw away or compost!

All it takes is a little knowledge of what each plant needs, and some time and attention to keep it growing strong.

COOL CARROT FOREST

MATERIALS

Wide-mouth half-pint (or pint-size) mason jar
Pebbles or glass marbles
Carrots (preferably with the tops still on)
Water

INSTRUCTIONS

1 Cut off the carrot greens (if any), then cut the carrots about 2 inches down from the crown (the top where the greens grow). Save these chunks but eat the rest of the carrot!

2 Arrange a layer of pebbles (or marbles) on the bottom of the jar and then set the carrot chunks, cut side down, on top.

3 Add water so the carrots are almost covered, and place the jar on a sunny windowsill.

What to Watch For

Keep an eye on the water level and add more if needed. Eventually small hairlike roots should start to appear along the sides and bottom of the carrot, and green fronds should pop from the top. To keep the plants going longer, transplant them to a bigger jar with potting mix.

What's Going On

Carrots are biennial, meaning they flower and produce seeds over two years. The first year, they store up food in their root. The second year, they grow a flower from that root. Setting the cut-off crown in water starts the carrot growing again for its second year. (So, no, it won't produce another carrot, but you might eventually see a flower!)

Super SWEET POTATO

MATERIALS

Wide-mouth mason jar large enough
for your sweet potato

Sweet potato

Toothpicks

Water

INSTRUCTIONS

1 Make sure that about two-thirds of the potato can fit in the jar, with the pointed end down. If both ends are pointed, look for the end marked with a round scar where the potato was attached to the plant. This end points up.

2 Insert two or three toothpicks into the potato so they hold the potato's lower end just above the bottom of the jar when they are resting on the jar's edge. Set the potato in the jar and fill it with water.

3 Set the jar on a sunny windowsill, and add more water whenever the level drops. Observe what happens.

What to Watch For

Within a week or two, you should see some small roots growing, followed by red sprouts on the top. The sprouts should eventually turn into long vines with lush foliage. When the vines are about 6 inches long, you can transplant the potato to a larger container with potting mix if you like.

If your potato does not grow roots, it may have been treated to keep it from sprouting, a common procedure on grocery store varieties. Try another, preferably one that's organic or from a local farm.

What's Going On

Sweet potatoes are tubers, a thickened underground stem where the plant stores food for the next growing season. When you expose the tuber to light and water, it starts growing, sending out new shoots called slips that can each become a new plant.

Once the potato slips are large enough, you can break them from the potato and set them in water. They will eventually grow their own roots and can be planted in a garden.

TELL ME MORE

You may have heard sweet potatoes referred to as yams, but in fact the two are entirely different vegetables. The true yam has a rough barklike skin and is usually white inside. The sweet potato has a smoother skin, and flesh that can be creamy white, bright orange, or even purple. When you see "yams" in the grocery store, they are most likely sweet potatoes. The confusion can be traced back to when growers of orange sweet potatoes first introduced them to consumers, and wanted to call them something that would distinguish them from the white-fleshed varieties.

73

Awesome AVOCADO TREE

It may take a few weeks for the sprout to grow.

MATERIALS

Pint-size (or larger) Mason jar. A wide-mouth jar makes transplanting easier.

Pit from an avocado

Knife (optional)

Potting mix

Plastic sandwich bag

Toothpicks or paper towels and ziplock bag

Water

INSTRUCTIONS

1 Wash off the pit and remove the brown skin, if you can, using your fingernail or a knife. (This helps germination but isn't essential.)

2 You now have several germination options. With three avocado pits, you can try all three methods and see which works the best!

Option 1: Plant It

The easiest method is to simply fill the jar about three-quarters full with potting mix and then sink the pit (pointy end up) into the soil. Leave about one-third of the pit uncovered, as avocados need light to germinate. Water it well, cover the jar with a plastic sandwich bag, and place it on a sunny windowsill. Remove the bag when a sprout appears.

Option 2: Soak It

To see more of what is going on, insert three toothpicks into the pit's upper half, each pointing slightly upward, then set the pit in a jar filled with water, with the toothpicks supporting it on the rim. The pit should be about half covered by the water. Place the jar on a sunny windowsill and keep an eye on the water level so the pit does not dry out.

Option 3: Wrap It

Wrap the pit in damp paper towels, place it in a sealed plastic ziplock bag, and set it on a warm, sunny windowsill. Check the pit weekly to make sure the towels are moist.

What to Watch For

Avocado pits can take several weeks or longer to germinate. Eventually the pit will crack and a sprout will emerge. If you are using the toothpick or paper towel method, transplant the germinated pit to a jar or small pot filled with potting mix, keeping at least half an inch of the pit above the soil line. After another few weeks, the sprout should grow taller and eventually produce leaves. Keep the soil moist and be patient!

TELL ME MORE

Given the right conditions, avocado trees started from pits can grow to be quite large, but they rarely produce fruit. Commercial growers instead rely on trees that have been grafted, meaning the roots from one variety of avocado have been joined to the trunk and branches of another variety known to produce fruit.

75

GRASS HEADS

Give your favorite scientist (or relative) a living head of hair.

OUR HAIR-LARIOUS TRIO: Bill Nye the Science Guy; astrophysicist Neil deGrasse Tyson (get it? de grass!); and physicist Albert Einstein

MATERIALS

- Pint-size mason jar
- Cheesecloth (available at the supermarket)
- Grass seed (we used cat grass seed for thicker hair)
- Potting mix
- Yarn or string
- Bowl of water
- Printed photograph of your favorite person

Grass and hair have three things in common: (1) both come in lots of varieties; (2) both need to be regularly trimmed; and (3) both are hard for some dads to grow! This project demonstrates that growing grass can be much easier than growing hair.

The secret is the cheesecloth wrap that holds the seeds and dirt: it also works as a wick to keep the seeds moist, a key requirement for germination. Once the grass is growing, you need to check the water level only once a week or so.

1 Cut a 1-foot by 2-foot section from the cheesecloth, then fold it in half to make a piece about a foot square. Place two or three tablespoons of seeds in the very center of the square. Use the jar to measure a half pint of potting mix. Pour it in a pile over the seeds.

2 Gather the four corners and twist the cloth to create a ball of soil, then tie off the ball with yarn or string. The ball should be just the right size to sit on the top of a pint jar. The excess cloth forms a wick that will draw water up to the soil.

3 Soak the ball and wick in the bowl of water and lightly squeeze out the excess. Fill the jar halfway up with water and place the ball on top with the wick hanging down.

4 Print out a famous face or a family snapshot so the image is roughly the height of the jar (about 5½ inches). Trim the photo so the top of the head is cut off. Tape the photo in place, lining up the forehead with the rim of the jar. Place the jar in a warm sunny spot.

CONTINUED →

What to Watch For

The wick will keep the ball of soil moist, but you may need to refill the jar after a few days (add the water at the sink after first carefully lifting up the soil ball). In a few days, roots should appear below the ball, then green shoots on top.

After a week or so, your jar should have a full head of hair. Feel free to give your grass head a haircut when needed.

Kids should be allowed to break stuff more often. That's a consequence of exploration. Exploration is what you do when you don't know what you're doing.

— Astrophysicist Neil deGrasse Tyson

Very Berry INK

Go old school and write with all-natural materials.

It's hard to imagine writing with a pen made from a bird's wing feather. But for more than a thousand years, up until the invention of the metal pen in the 1820s, that's the way it was done. To write with a quill pen, you have to first dip it in ink and, over the centuries, science-minded ink makers have come up with elaborate recipes using plants, minerals, and even animal parts. Here, we use berries with a few other key ingredients. To test it out, make a pen from a plastic drinking straw.

MATERIALS

2 half-pint (or larger) mason jars, one with two-piece lid

½ cup ripe berries, such as blueberries, blackberries, strawberries, elderberries, or raspberries; it's fine to use the ones that are overripe and not good for eating.

Small mesh strainer

Spoon

½ teaspoon vinegar

½ teaspoon sea salt

Plastic straw

Scissors

CONTINUED →

INSTRUCTIONS

To make the ink

1 Place the berries in one of the jars, cover it with a paper towel, and microwave for 30 to 60 seconds, until the berries are softened and juicy.

2 Working in batches, press the berries through the strainer with the back of a spoon, mashing them over the other jar to collect the juice. Compost or throw away the leftover pulp.

3 Add the vinegar and salt to the juice, and stir until the salt dissolves.

4 Cover the mason jar and keep it refrigerated. The ink will work even better after sitting overnight.

To make the pen

1 Cut the straw at an angle to create a point, then cut off the very end of the point to create a flat writing tip.

2 Cut a half-inch-long slit from the tip into the tube of the straw.

3 Dip the straw in the ink and gently write on a piece of paper. Dip whenever you need more ink.

What to Watch For

If the ink is too thick, thin it with water, adding just a little at a time, until the consistency is smoother and the ink flows the way you want. Don't add too much! You'll dilute the color.

What's Going On

What makes berries so good for ink (and so good for us!) are pigments known as anthocyanins (for more, see Red Cabbage Chemistry Set, page 26), which give them their distinct red, blue, or purple color. The acidic vinegar in this recipe serves as a fixative, a substance that makes the pigments more permanent. The salt prevents mold from growing.

The juice travels down the split in the pen and onto the paper through capillary action (see Walking Watercolors, page 108). In an actual quill pen, the tip, or nib, is heat-treated for strength and then carefully carved to give the writer better control of the ink flow. Every few pages, the writer needs to sharpen the nib using a penknife (yes, that's where they got that name!).

TELL ME MORE

Any hard, pointed object can be dipped in ink and used to write. But ancient people soon discovered that a sharpened hollow tube — such as a reed straw — held more ink and required less dipping. Quills from large birds proved even better for writing, and became the state-of-the-art tool from the sixth century until the early 1800s.

Thomas Jefferson, who wrote the Declaration of Independence with a quill pen, raised special geese at his farm, Monticello, so he would always have a supply of quills on hand. Only the first few feathers from the bird's left wing were used, as the curve allowed right-handed people to see their work (writing left-handed was discouraged; it smudged the ink).

Given the effort of using quill pens, it's not surprising that Jefferson bought a fountain pen as soon as he saw one in 1824. He paid $5, the equivalent of about $100 today. Made of silver and gold, it was "one of the best I ever saw," he wrote.

Seedling
SUPERMAN!

Train a baby plant to pump iron.

Puppies and kittens are cute and cuddly, but if you like your babies strong, look at plants. A seed has to fend for itself from the moment it gets flung on the ground. If the temperature and moisture conditions are right for germinating, it has to sink its roots in the soil and pop out leaves fast, before the conditions change. That takes strength, as you can see in this experiment, where a bean seed shows that it can actually lift weights!

MATERIALS

Half-pint (or pint-size) mason jar

Potting mix

Bean seed (we used a green bean)

4 toothpicks

Penny

Plastic sandwich bag

Water

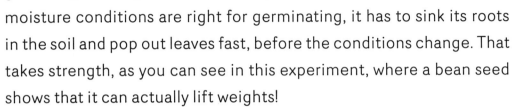
INSTRUCTIONS

1 Fill the jar with potting mix. Plant a bean seed in the center of the jar, about half an inch deep. Water it well without making the soil soggy.

2 Place a penny on the soil over the bean and set four toothpicks around the penny, as shown below.

3 Place the jar in a warm, sunny spot, covered with a small plastic bag to keep the soil moist. When the bean starts to sprout, you can remove the bag.

What to Watch For

The bean can take from just a few days to more than a week to germinate, but once it does, it grows quickly! If the penny is pushed aside, adjust the toothpicks and set it back in place. Check the soil every few days and add water if it dries out. If the bean does not germinate, try another. (For more, see Root View, page 68.)

What's Going On

The bean seed first puts out a main root called the radical. The radical grows downward to anchor the seedling and begins absorbing water. Next the seed sends up a stem (called a hypocotyl) with seed-shaped leaves (cotyledons), and, finally, puts out its true leaves. The seedling grows with enough force to push away objects that might be in its way, such as pebbles, sticks, leaves, and even pennies!

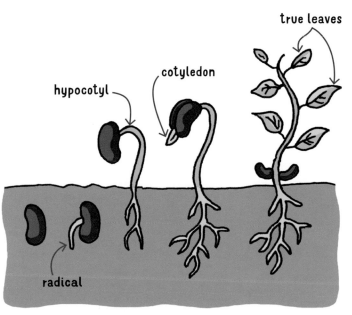

hypocotyl

cotyledon

true leaves

radical

TAKE IT FURTHER

After your bean has done its weightlifting, make it do sit-ups! Carefully remove the seedling from the mason jar (using a table fork can help), and transplant it to a larger rectangular pot, pressing the new potting mix firmly in place. Water the mix well, and then place the pot in a sunny window, set down on its side. Keep the soil moist, and watch what happens over the next few days. Rather than grow sideways, the seedling should start to turn and grow upward toward the light, a process called phototropism.

IT'S ALIVE!
BIOLOGY

Biology is the study of living things, from the microscopic bacteria that live inside us to the massive whales that roam the oceans. People, plants, animals, insects, and bacteria might seem different, but to the biologist, they are all members of the same special club. That's because all living things are made up of cells, the building blocks of life.

Starting at this very basic level, biologists study how life works, how living things reproduce, why they get sick, and how they grow. They closely observe the natural world and its amazing creatures, exploring the many ways that living things manage to survive. The projects on the following pages let you observe the living world for yourself. Treat your small guests with respect. After all, you have a lot in common.

Make a
BUG VACUUM

This simple device lets you capture insects with ease.

Scientists capture bugs for study using a mouth-powered vacuum, called an aspirator or a pooter. Swallowing your specimens isn't good science, so this device is specially designed so bugs are sucked into the chamber, not into your mouth! You can make your own version from a mason jar. Use it to gather ants (or other small insects) and then observe them in action.

MATERIALS

Pint-size mason jar with two-piece lid

Milk or juice carton

Hole punch

2 bendy straws

Tape

Gauze pad

INSTRUCTIONS

1 Open the milk carton along the seams and flatten it out. Use the inner lid of the mason jar as a template to trace a circle on the carton. Cut out the circle and punch two holes in the center about an inch apart.

2 Carefully slide the short ends of the bendy straws into the holes. Tape a piece of gauze pad around the end of one straw to prevent any bugs from getting sucked up.

bug intake tube

air intake tube

bug stopping mechanism

TELL ME MORE

Ants were the Earth's first farmers. For millions of years, certain species have been creating underground gardens where they grow their favorite fungus for food. They tend to their crops, bringing them water and even weeding out other fungi they don't want.

3 Set the lid on the jar and fasten it in place with the ring.

4 To use your pooter, place the tip of the straw without the gauze near a bug. Put your mouth on the straw with the gauze, and gently suck in. The bug should travel up the straw and land unharmed at the bottom of the jar.

Take It Further

Capture some ants in your bug vacuum, then use a magnifying glass to observe these remarkable insects up close. Open the jar and feed them a few drops of sugary water or corn syrup, or try giving them some birdseed. Ants live in colonies headed by a queen ant, and they can't last long on their own. When you are done observing them, release your ants where you found them. (Note: Some ants bite, so be careful handling them.)

SCIENCE iN REAL LiFE

A design for a mouth-powered bug vacuum similar to this one was first described in a 1929 scientific paper by American entomologist (a scientist who studies insects) Frederick William Poos, Jr. (1891-1987), who had developed it for catching leafhoppers. On the sucking end of the intake tube, Poos used a fancy cigarette holder for a mouthpiece. On the tube's other end, he placed a silk filter to keep bugs out of his mouth. Poos's gadget was not the first bug vacuum, but his design has stuck around, along with a nickname that pays tribute to its inventor: entomologists call it a pooter.

HUMMING FEEDER

Attract these tiny visitors with a flowery sweet treat.

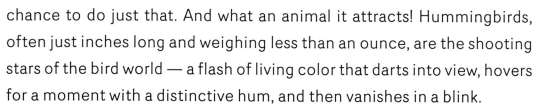

Nature may look good on television, but nothing compares to seeing an animal up close with your own eyes. This simple feeder gives you a chance to do just that. And what an animal it attracts! Hummingbirds, often just inches long and weighing less than an ounce, are the shooting stars of the bird world — a flash of living color that darts into view, hovers for a moment with a distinctive hum, and then vanishes in a blink.

Persuading these miniature marvels to stick around your yard takes strategy, patience, and a little luck. Start by offering them a favorite treat: sugary water served in a mason jar feeder, with a side of fake flowers to attract them. Then keep your eyes (and ears!) open for their arrival.

MATERIALS

FOR THE FEEDER

Half-pint mason jar with two-piece lid

Plastic lid from a butter or yogurt tub, preferably red

Hole punch

5 to 10 red waterproof artificial flowers

Rubber band

Bendable wire, about 2 feet long

FOR THE SYRUP

Pint-size mason jar with two-piece lid

¼ cup cane sugar (do not use brown sugar, honey, or any other sweetener, as these are not healthy for hummingbirds)

1 cup water

SAFETY FIRST: This experiment involves using a microwave and should be done with adult supervision. Use potholders to handle hot jars.

1 Use the inner lid as a template to cut a circle from the plastic lid. Punch three holes in the center of the circle. Set the circle inside the screw-on ring.

2 Wrap the wire around the neck of the jar, between the glass ridges, and twist it tightly to itself, to serve as a hanger. When the feeder is hanging, the jar should tilt at a slight angle, but not so much that the syrup spills out.

3 Stretch the rubber band around the jar near the mouth (if the band is too big, twist and loop it so it's tight). Trim the flower stems so they are an inch or so long, then arrange the flowers around the mouth of the jar, tucking the stems under the rubber band.

4 Make the syrup: stir all the ingredients together in the pint mason jar and microwave it for about 2 minutes to dissolve the sugar. Using potholders, carefully remove the syrup and let it cool.

5 Fill the feeder half full and screw on the top. Hang it outside from a pole, tree branch, or other structure, at least 4 feet above the ground, and in a shady spot near other red flowers, if possible.

CONTINUED →

What to Watch For

Hummingbirds are attracted to bright colors, especially red. Once they know a feeder is nearby, they often make a habit of coming by for a meal, and will remember a good food supply from year to year.

Unfortunately, bugs and bees are also attracted to the sweet syrup, so check the feeder and thoroughly clean it out and refill it every 4 to 5 days (more often in hot weather). Use warm, soapy water and rinse it thoroughly. A dirty or moldy feeder is not good for the birds!

TELL ME MORE

You can't see them do it unless you have a slow-motion camera, but hummingbirds flap their wings in a figure-eight pattern, as fast as 80 times a second! This allows them to hover in midair as they feed, and also what creates that distinctive humming sound.

Flying this way uses a lot of energy, so every day they have to eat one to two times their body weight in nectar, along with bugs for protein!

CRITTER CONTAINERS

You may not think of insects as impressive pets, but spend some time observing them and you may change your mind. Earthworms work like pooping machines to turn rotting leaves into rich garden soil. Crickets are musicians whose chirping pattern lets you know how warm it is. Caterpillars transform themselves like superheroes into moths and butterflies.

Get to know each of these insects better with the help of a customized critter observation chamber made from a mason jar. As suited as each jar is to its insect guest, it's still just a temporary home. So be sure to release your insects when you are done.

Worm COMPOSTER

MATERIALS

Wide-mouth quart-size mason jar with two-piece lid

12-ounce jar, aluminum can, or other narrow container that fits inside the quart jar

¾–1 cup garden soil

½ cup light sandy soil

Stiff paper and pushpin

Construction paper and tape

Chopped veggie scraps for food

Water

INSTRUCTIONS

1 Set the smaller container upside down inside the larger jar. This forces the worms to tunnel near the outer glass, where you can observe them.

2 Add a few spoonfuls of garden soil to the jar, pouring it evenly around the sides so it fills in the space between the two jars and creates a layer about an inch deep. If the soil is not moist, add a little water.

3 Add a thin layer of sandy soil, then another 1-inch layer of garden soil, then a thin layer of sandy soil, and so on, until you've nearly filled the jar,

topping it with darker garden soil. The thin layers of sandy soil will allow you to see how the tunneling worms mix soils together.

4 To make a perforated cover for the jar, use the inner lid to trace a circle on the paper. Cut it out and poke several dozen holes in it with the pushpin. Set it inside the screw-on ring in place of the inner lid.

5 Gather your earthworms. Dig in a garden bed or in your compost pile, or look under rotting logs or piles of leaves (worms need dark, moist living conditions). An even easier way is to go out after a rainstorm and rescue worms from the sidewalk!

6 Place about six worms in the jar and add some chopped veggie scraps for food, setting the scraps on top of the soil. Screw on the cover.

7 Wrap the jar with the construction paper and secure it with tape. This keeps the worms in the dark, where they like to be. Place the jar in a cool place, out of the sun (if you have one, a basement is ideal).

The construction paper sleeve keeps the jars dark, so worms will tunnel near the glass.

8 Sprinkle the surface with water every few days to keep everything moist. Slide off the paper wrapping after a day or two to see what the worms have done.

What to Watch For

Earthworms play a key role in the ecosystem of the soil. By eating food on the surface, bringing it into the soil, and producing poop (called castings), they make the soil more fertile for plants. Their tunneling mixes the soil and allows in air and water, which also helps plants. You should be able to see the effects of their tunneling after a few days. Notice the changes in the layers of lighter and darker soils, and how food that was once on the surface is now gone.

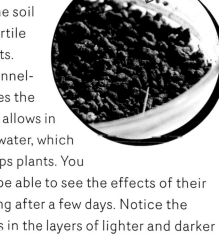

worm castings

TELL ME MORE

You would need a much bigger jar to hold a Giant Gippsland earthworm (*Megascolides australis*). Native to Australia, they can grow to be 10 feet long! This rare and protected species lives deep underground, but heavy rains can sometimes force them to the surface.

Cricket CONCERT HALL

Only male crickets chirp. They make the sound by rubbing their wings together.

MATERIALS

Wide-mouth quart-size (or larger) mason jar with two-piece lid

Stiff paper and pushpin

Scissors

Sand or soil, leaves, sticks, rocks, and a section of cardboard egg carton

Tweezers

Carton cap and cotton ball (for water)

Various food scraps (cereal, lettuce, fruit, birdseed)

Water

Small jar or plastic cup and thin cardboard

INSTRUCTIONS

1 To make a perforated cover for the jar, use the inner lid to trace a circle on the paper. Cut it out and poke several dozen holes in it with the pushpin. Set it inside the screw-on ring in place of the inner lid.

2 Add a layer of moist sand or dirt to the bottom of the jar, along with other things crickets like: leaves, rocks, sticks, a section of egg carton to hide under, and so on. Use tweezers to set items in place.

3 Prepare a watering station: soak a cotton ball in water, set it in a carton cap, and place the cap in the jar.

4 Find your cricket! Look for the common black field cricket (known to scientists as *Gryllus assimilis*; for more on scientific names, see Categorizing a Cricket, page 45) outside under rocks or logs, or in grassy areas. In the fall, they often come inside houses looking for a warm spot, and if it's a male, you will hear it loudly chirping (the sound is actually the cricket rubbing its wings together).

Use a jar or plastic cup to catch it: quickly set the jar over the cricket, then slide a piece of thin cardboard under the jar to seal the cricket in. Another common species is the brown house cricket (*Acheta domesticus*), which you can buy in bait and pet stores (it's a food for lizards and snakes).

What to Watch For

A cricket will eat almost anything. Try giving it small bits of fruit or vegetables, and keep the cotton ball moist as a source of water. If you are keeping your cricket longer than a few days, clean out the cage every 2 or 3 days.

If you happen to find two crickets and both are male (females have a long, pointed egg-laying "tail" called an ovipositor), don't put them together in the same jar, as they will fight to the death! Keep the jar in a cool spot, out of the sunlight.

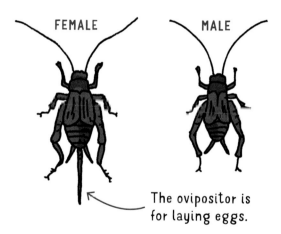

FEMALE   MALE

The ovipositor is for laying eggs.

TELL ME MORE

For centuries, crickets have been prized as pets in China and Japan, where they are raised for fighting and kept in special containers and cages so their chirping can be heard. Because crickets chirp faster when it's warmer, an old bit of country wisdom says you can estimate the temperature (in Fahrenheit) by counting the number of chirps in 14 seconds, then adding 40 to that number. So if you counted 35 chirps in 14 seconds, the temperature would be 75°F.

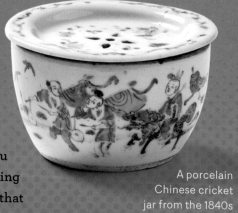

A porcelain Chinese cricket jar from the 1840s

Caterpillar DINER

MATERIALS

- Quart-size (or larger) mason jar with two-piece lid
- Stiff paper and pushpin
- Scissors
- Paper towels
- Sticks or twigs
- Leaves from the plant you found your caterpillar on

INSTRUCTIONS

1 To make a perforated cover for the jar, use the inner lid to trace a circle on the paper. Cut it out and poke several dozen holes in it with the pushpin. Set it inside the screw-on ring in place of the inner lid.

2 Moisten a paper towel and set it at the bottom of the jar to provide some humidity for your caterpillar guest. Add leaves or other natural materials to cover the paper towel.

The furry black-and-brown-banded caterpillars known as woolly bears (*Pyrrharctia isabella*) are the larvae of the Isabella Tiger Moth. Found throughout the United States, they are seen most often in the fall, when they move about in search of a place to hibernate. According to folklore (which is not science!), the more black in woolly bear bands, the harsher the winter will be.

3 Find your caterpillar! If your family or a neighbor has a garden, ask if you can look for caterpillars on the plants.

4 When you find a caterpillar, remove the whole leaf or stem that you found it on, as that is what it needs to eat. Place the leaf and the caterpillar in the jar, and screw on the lid.

What to Watch For

Caterpillars, which are the larvae of butterflies and moths, tend to eat specific plants, so if you plan to keep your caterpillar for a while, you'll need to give it more leaves from the plant you found it on. Knowing what it eats can also help you identify which kind of caterpillar it is (use a reference book or look online to find species that are common where you live).

Eventually, the caterpillar stops eating, attaches itself to a twig (or drops to the ground), and forms a pupa. Sometime later, depending on the species, the pupa's shell cracks and the new butterfly or moth emerges, slowly unfolds its wings, and flies off. This process is called metamorphosis.

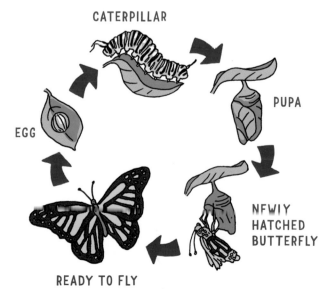

CATERPILLAR

PUPA

NEWLY HATCHED BUTTERFLY

READY TO FLY

EGG

TELL ME MORE

The caterpillars of the monarch butterfly feed entirely on milkweed plants, a common weed in the United States. In the fall, the adult butterflies pull off one of the most remarkable feats of insect athleticism, migrating thousands of miles to warmer climates!

Monarchs in the eastern United States fly all the way to Mexico. Monarchs in the western United States migrate to Pacific Grove, California, and other sites, where they color the trees with their distinctive orange and black wings.

The Incredible
(INEDIBLE) EGG

Turn an egg into a rubbery blob that shrinks and expands.

Dissolve an egg's shell in a jar of vinegar and you end up with a blob that is something between a water balloon and a jellyfish. But as delightfully creepy as a shell-less egg is, making it is just the beginning of the fun. By soaking your blob in various other fluids, you can grow it and shrink it to have a firsthand look at osmosis, the process your body uses to move water to where it is most needed.

MATERIALS

Wide-mouth pint-size mason jar
Raw egg
1½ cups vinegar

INSTRUCTIONS

1 Carefully place the egg in the jar and add the vinegar. Keep the jar uncovered to let the gas escape.

2 Observe the changes over the next few days.

What to Watch For

The shell should soon be covered in bubbles. By the next day, the shell should start to dissolve, creating some scum at the surface. When the shell is mostly gone (usually after a few days), carefully remove the egg and rinse off any remaining bits of shell. If the shell doesn't all come off, put it back in the jar with fresh vinegar for another day or two. Does the egg look larger? Hold it in your hand but don't squeeze too hard! And although you probably wouldn't consider it, don't eat the egg.

What's Going On

Vinegar contains acid, specifically acetic acid. Eggshells (like seashells) are made of calcium carbonate. When the two are combined, they react. As the eggshell dissolves, carbon dioxide is produced, which explains the bubbles. The egg expands as water seeps through its rubbery inner skin, or membrane. More specifically, this is a semi-permeable membrane, which means it lets water pass through it but holds back other materials, like a window screen that lets in air but keeps out bugs. Similar membranes are also found in our cells and elsewhere in our bodies, so they are of great interest to biologists. To see how a membrane works, try the experiments in Take It Further, below!

TAKE IT FURTHER

Soak your shell-less egg in a jar of water overnight and see what happens. (It should swell up even larger.) Place your egg in a jar of thick corn syrup, and it should eventually shrivel up into a loose sack. Both outcomes happen because the egg's semi-permeable membrane allows water to pass from the more watery side to the less watery one.

When you place the egg in pure water, the membrane allows water to flow into the egg (where there is less water), and the egg expands.

Place the egg in corn syrup (which contains little water), and the water flows the other way, causing the egg to shrivel. This process is known as osmosis, and living things depend on it as a way to move water in and out of cells and wherever else it's needed. Egg-straordinary!

Swollen from water

Shriveled from corn syrup

WATER

CORN SYRUP

PICKLE FACTORY

Watch good bacteria turn cucumbers into pickles.

You don't have to be a biologist to love sour pickles, but knowing the science behind them can make you appreciate them even more. Don't confuse these homemade pickles with the ones you see on the store shelves, packed in vinegar and sealed tight. These pickles are literally alive! They get their flavor from millions of good bacteria, and the sourness changes the longer the bacteria work on them. Depending on the temperature, the process takes from a few days to a week.

But here's the best part: not only are they good to eat, but they're healthy, too. That's a good kind of pickle to be in!

MATERIALS

Quart-size mason jar

Wide-mouth 2-quart (or larger) mason jar with lid

Pint-size or half-pint mason jar (narrow enough to fit in the mouth of the larger jar)

Small pickling cucumbers (about 2 pounds, or enough to fill the jar)

2 tablespoons sea salt

1 quart of water

Wooden spoon

8 or so cloves of garlic, chopped into chunks

2 or 3 dill heads*

10 whole peppercorns

*These are the branched seedpods of the dill plant. If you can't find these, substitute about 1 tablespoon of chopped fresh dill and 1 tablespoon dill seeds.

INSTRUCTIONS

1 Rinse off the cucumbers. Give the blossom end (the one that wasn't attached to the vine) a good scrubbing to get rid of any bits of blossom, which can make pickles mushy.

2 Fill the quart jar with water and add the salt. Stir until the salt dissolves. This salty solution is called a brine. You may not use all of it, but don't adjust the amount of salt or water, as the ratio (the amount of each ingredient in relation to the others) is very important.

3 Place the garlic chunks, the dill, and the peppercorns at the bottom of the 2-quart jar. Add the cucumbers, stacking them neatly so you can fit in as many as possible.

4 Fill the jar with the brine, stopping about an inch from the top.

5 Insert the smaller jar into the mouth of the larger jar so it presses the cucumbers below the surface of the brine. You want to keep your pickles submerged at all times. Add some brine to the small jar if it isn't heavy enough to press down the pickles.

6 Set the jar in a cool spot (70–75°F/ 21–24°C is ideal), on a plate (for any spills), and out of sunlight. Cover the jars with a dish towel to keep out bugs and dust.

CONTINUED →

What to Watch For

Observe your pickles over the next few days. Look for changes in the color of the cucumbers, and for changes in the brine. When you gently press down on the smaller jar, you might see bubbles rise in the brine. Give the jar a sniff. How does it smell?

After 3 or so days, pull out a pickle to sample. Cut it in half. What do you notice about the inside of the cucumber? Taste it.

If you like the level of sourness, cover the jar with the lid and put it in the refrigerator to stop the pickling process. If not, let the jar sit out a few days longer.

What's Going On

What you've been observing is the process known as fermentation. Microscopic bacteria on the surface of the cucumbers, mostly a variety called lactobacillus, have been hard at work, transforming the sugar in the cucumbers into lactic acid, alcohol, and carbon dioxide gas. That bubbling you see is the carbon dioxide gas, and that sourness you taste is the lactic acid (and other flavors from the herbs and spices).

The salt in the brine allows the good lactobacillus bacteria to thrive, while making life hard for other bad bacteria that would spoil the pickles. That's why the amount of salt in your brine is so important: too much and even the good bacteria can't survive. Not enough, and the bad ones will take over. (Something isn't right if your pickles start to smell yeasty or turn pink. If they do, toss them.)

The salt also makes the pickles hard and crunchy by drawing out water through osmosis (see The Incredible [Inedible] Egg, page 98).

Note: Keep an eye on your room temperature. If it's much hotter than 75°F/24°C, the lactobacillus are not as happy, and other microbes might take over.

TELL ME MORE

Fermenting is one of humanity's oldest food preservation techniques. Before the invention of refrigeration, it gave people a way to set aside food for the winter or for times when other food was scarce. As far back as 2,000 years ago, workers building the Great Wall of China ate fermented cabbage!

THE YEAST YOU COULD DO

Put a few billion creatures to work blowing up a balloon.

You probably know that yeast is what makes bread rise, but you might not really understand just how that works. Or rather, how *they* work. A package of yeast isn't one thing. It's billions of things — living things. As soon as these single-cell creatures are exposed to warm liquid and sugar, they burst to life, digesting that sugar and putting out carbon dioxide gas. That gas is what forms the bubbles in bread dough and makes the loaf rise. You can use that same gas to blow up a balloon!

MATERIALS

- Pint-size mason jar
- Balloon
- Jar spout (see page 105)
- 1 cup warm tap water
- Spoonful of sugar or honey
- Active dry yeast, ¼-ounce packet

INSTRUCTIONS

1 Blow up the balloon to stretch it out, and then let the air out. Place the neck of the stretched-out balloon over the jar spout.

2 Add the warm tap water to the pint jar, and then add a spoonful of sugar or honey. (To test the temperature, dip your fingers in the water — it shouldn't feel hot or cold.)

3 Sprinkle the yeast onto the water, and give it all a good stir.

4 Screw on the spout with the balloon attached and twist the ring extra tight to create a good seal. Watch what happens during the next 10 minutes.

CONTINUED →

What to Watch For

If the yeast doesn't start to bubble in a few minutes, the water may be too hot or too cold, or the yeast may be old. If the yeast is bubbling but the balloon isn't inflating, the spout may not be tightly sealed, so give it another turn.

What's Going On

Yeast are actually single-celled fungi, and they are everywhere: in the air, on fruits and vegetables, and even living on us. Baker's yeast is a special strain used for cooking. When given warm water and sugar, the yeast quickly begin growing and feeding, starting a process called fermentation, the same process that gives us sour pickles (see Pickle Factory, page 100), as well as beer and wine. Fermentation also produces carbon dioxide gas. Eventually, the yeast should produce enough gas to lift up the balloon.

SCIENCE IN REAL LIFE

SCIENCE IN REAL LIFE

Bakers knead bread dough to make it rubbery and elastic. This allows it to better trap the bubbles of gas given off by the yeast and hold them in the dough while the bread bakes. It's like having hundreds of tiny balloons in every loaf!

Take It Further

Use your gas catcher to observe an even more powerful carbon dioxide–producing reaction: baking soda and vinegar. (This reaction can be so powerful, in fact, that you'll want to do it in a sink or outside, just in case the balloon comes loose.)

With the lid off and the balloon attached to the jar spout, carefully spoon about 2 tablespoons of baking soda through the spout into the balloon. Add about 4 ounces of white vinegar to the jar. Pinch the neck of the balloon to hold the baking soda inside, then tightly screw the spout on the jar. Once the spout is on, lift the balloon so the baking soda pours into the vinegar, and watch what happens!

TELL ME MORE

Each ¼-ounce package of yeast contains 140,000,000,000 (that's 140 billion!) individual yeast cells. The scientific name for the baking variety is *Saccharomyces cerevisiae*, which means "sugar-eating fungus."

JAR SPOUT

To make this handy lid, you'll need a carton with a built-in plastic spout, the kind that milk and juice come in.

SAFETY FIRST: Some spout caps have sharp points for cutting through the seal when you twist them open. Watch out for them when you flatten out the top!

1 Rinse the carton and drain it thoroughly. Cut off the bottom half.

2 Press open the seams that form the top. Cut along the side seam, so the carton is now flat.

3 Use a mason jar ring as a template to draw a circle around the spout.

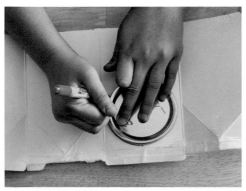

4 Cut along the circle and then press the circle into the ring. Trim it to fit.

5 Screw the spout onto a jar and tighten it to create a seal.

UNDERSTANDING MATTER IN MOTION
PHYSICS

Everything in the universe is in motion. Some things move too slow for us to notice (such as the shifting of the earth's continents), others too fast for us to see (such as the beam of light from a lamp), but all moving things follow certain laws and are affected by natural forces, such as gravity. The field of science that helps us understand how all these moving things interact is called physics.

Famous scientists such as Sir Isaac Newton and Albert Einstein used physics to explore big questions like how the planets move and how the universe formed, but scientists also use physics to answer more basic questions about things such as heat, light, and electricity. Engineers, for example, would not be able to design skyscrapers or smart phones without it. You can see the laws of physics at work in the following activities, where things are made to move in some very surprising ways.

Walking WATER-COLORS

Make colored water move from jar to jar.

Sometimes science seems like magic, as it does in this experiment. How can water flow uphill and over the edge of a jar? What happened to gravity? The answer is capillary action, which you've experienced if you've ever accidentally stepped in a deep puddle and later felt the water slowly climbing up your pants. Here, that same force moves the colored water from one jar to another. As a bonus, you get to see another bit of science magic: how three colors can become six.

MATERIALS

7 half-pint (or pint-size) mason jars

Food coloring

Water

Paper towels

INSTRUCTIONS

1 Fill four jars with water. With the food coloring, color two of them red, one blue, and one yellow. We used 10 drops in each.

2 Arrange the jars in the following pattern: red, empty, blue, empty, yellow, empty, red.

3 Roll six sheets of paper towel into wicks about an inch wide, and then fold them in half. Carefully place one end of each wick in a jar, as shown.

RED   Empty   BLUE   Empty   YELLOW   Empty   RED

What to Watch For

After a few minutes, the water from the full jars will climb up the wick and start flowing into the empty jars. Watch what happens when the colors start to mix. What do you notice about the amount of water in each jar when the process stops?

Red, blue, and yellow are called the primary colors because with careful mixing of just those three, you can create all the other shades. That's how your computer printer can create every color from just three inks (with ink, blue is called cyan, and red is magenta). Experiment with how you set up your wicking jars to see which new colors you can create!

What's Going On

The water rises up the paper towel because of capillary action, the same process that explains how the hairs of a paintbrush soak up paint, how plants draw water up through their stems, and how a polypropylene sports shirt wicks sweat away from your skin. Water wants to stick to things, a force called adhesion. It also wants to stick to itself, a force called cohesion.

Those forces make water flow into narrow spaces (such as into the air pockets of a paper towel) and are so strong that they can overcome gravity for a short distance. Once the water wicks its way over the high point of the paper towel, gravity takes over and the water flows down the other side, stopping when the level in each jar is the same.

TOWER OF LIQUIDS

Create a layered liquid rainbow.

Almost anyone can make a tower of blocks, but it takes a scientist to make a tower of liquids. That's because stacking liquids requires that you know something about density. The liquids here all have different densities, so they don't mix, and they are arranged in order, with the most dense on the bottom.

INSTRUCTIONS

1 Place an equal amount of liquid in each of the smaller jars (except for the honey, which is easier to add right from its container). We used 4 ounces of each to fill a quart jar.

2 Carefully pour a layer of honey into the bottom of the jar. Try to avoid getting any on the sides so you can see the other layers better.

3 Add the corn syrup by holding a spatula or long-handled spoon inside the jar and pouring the liquid over it. This method makes the corn syrup land more gently and prevents the layers from mixing.

4 Add the milk, soap, water, and oil using a turkey baster, syringe, or eyedropper, slowly adding the liquids in small amounts to avoid mixing the layers. Try dribbling the liquid down the side of the jar rather than down the center. Rinse the tool before adding a new layer to avoid contamination. These layers take patience!

What to Watch For

If some layers look at first like they have mixed, don't worry. After a few minutes they should separate. When you are done, you should have a neatly stacked tower of variously colored liquids.

Take It Further

Gather various small objects made of different materials, such as a metal screw, a large button, a grape, and a Ping-Pong ball. Once your layers are stable, gently drop one object at a time into the jar and observe what happens. Each object will sink until it reaches the level of liquid that has a greater level of density than it does.

What's Going On

The layers in the tower stay separate because they have been stacked according to their density. Density is not the same as weight, but it's related: it's how heavy a thing is combined with how big it is. So a small thing that weighs a lot, such as a gold coin, is dense, while a large thing that's light, such as Styrofoam, is not. If two things are the same size, the heavier one is more dense.

The density of a solid object determines if it will sink or float in a liquid. And as the Tower of Liquids shows, less dense liquids float on top of more dense ones.

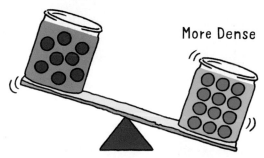

Less Dense

More Dense

Balloon
VACUUM

Demonstrate the effect of temperature on gases.

Have you ever closed the refrigerator door, then remembered that you needed something else and immediately tried to open the door again, only to have the door resist as you pull? Or maybe you've tried to open a sealed tub of leftovers and noticed that the lid was stuck onto the container? This experiment explains why. It all has to do with hot air.

Quart-size mason jar

Balloon

Hot tap water

INSTRUCTIONS

1 Blow up the balloon so it's an inch or so wider than the jar's mouth and tie it off.

2 Heat the jar by filling it with hot tap water and then microwaving it for a minute or so. Using potholders or gloves, pour out the hot water and set the jar on the counter.

3 Place the balloon over the jar's mouth, pressing lightly so it forms a seal all around. In a few seconds it should feel "stuck" and you can release your hold. Over the next 10 minutes, watch as the bottom of the balloon is drawn into the jar. Now try lifting the ballon.

What's Going On

If you've ever seen a hot air balloon take off, you know that when air is heated, it rises and expands. The opposite is also true: when hot air cools, it sinks and shrinks. The cooling, shrink-ing air creates low pressure inside the jar, and the sur-rounding higher pressure then pushes the balloon down (for more about air pressure, see Balloon Barometer, page 55.)

A similar thing happens when you open the fridge door. Warm air gets inside and starts to cool down. If your fridge has a tight seal, the door is hard to open until the air pressure equalizes.

SCIENCE IN REAL LIFE

Mason jars also use this phenome-non to preserve food. Their lids are lined with rubber for an airtight seal that keeps out contaminants. When you boil food or liquids in the lidded jars and then let the jars cool, the pressure inside the jar is lower than the surrounding air pressure, so the lids are pressed in place.

You can check this out by heating the jar, then screwing a new two-piece canning lid in place. Let the jar cool. Unscrew the band and try to remove the lid. What happens?

Light BENDER

Create a rainbow and make objects disappear with a jar of water.

Put a small mirror in an ordinary jar of water and you can create a remarkable scientific instrument: a lens that can bend and split light. Like a prism, the device turns ordinary sunlight into the colors of the rainbow. A jar filled with water can also make a coin seem to disappear. The secret again: bending light.

MATERIALS

- Any size mason jar, preferably with smooth sides, with two-piece lid
- A rectangular mirror narrow enough to fit inside the jar (ours is 2¼ by 3¾ inches)
- Water
- A sheet of white paper
- Sunlight (preferably early morning or evening light)

INSTRUCTIONS

1 Set the mirror in the jar so it rests at an angle, and then add water until the mirror is halfway submerged.

2 Find a spot where morning or evening sun comes through a window. Place the jar on the floor in the beam of sunlight so the mirror reflects the rays back toward the window. (Note: if you don't have a sunny spot, try using a strong flashlight in a darkened room.)

3 Holding the sheet of paper, catch the reflected beam of light. Move the paper back several feet so the reflection grows larger. Look closely at the colors around the edges of the reflected light.

What to Watch For

You may have to adjust the position of the jar and the paper, but if the beam of light is bright enough the device should create a narrow band of colors on the paper. As you move the paper farther from the jar, the band will get larger, revealing the colors of the rainbow.

What's Going On

A beam of sunlight may look like it's just white light, but it's actually made up of many colors, each one with a different wavelength. When light passes through air into another substance, in this case the jar of water, it bends, a phenomenon known as refraction. The various wavelengths within the light bend at different angles, which makes them spread out into their various colors (something called dispersion), sort of like fanning a deck of cards. The mirror helps amplify this effect.

TAKE IT FURTHER

Remove the mirror from the jar, fill it with water, and screw on the lid. Place a penny on a table, then set the jar on top of it. Hey, where did the coin go? See if you can spot it by looking from various angles. Still no luck?

The reason has to do with refraction again. The water and the jar refract your view of the penny, making it seem to disappear. Remove the lid and look down into the jar. There it is!

Now you can't see it . . .

Now you can!

115

HERON'S FOUNTAIN

Build a water bubbler powered by the pull of gravity.

Some 2,000 years ago, the famous Greek scientist and engineer, Heron (or Hero) of Alexandria, invented a water fountain powered just by gravity — no pumps required! He used it to demonstrate the laws of moving liquids (hydraulics) and gases (pneumatics). You can witness those same forces at work in this simplified version.

MATERIALS

Pint-size mason jar with two-piece lid

Quart-size (or larger) mason jar

Waterproof carton (juice box or milk carton)

Hole punch

3 straws

Duct tape or other waterproof tape

Water

1 Use the inner lid as a template to draw a circle on the carton, and cut it out. Check to make sure it fits inside the ring.

2 Punch two holes in the circle, as shown. Make a long straw by pinching the end of one straw, inserting it into the end of another one, and taping the joint.

3 Test to see how your straws fit through the holes in the circle. If they don't fit snugly, wrap a layer of tape around each straw to form a better seal. Wrap the short straw 3½ inches from the end. Wrap the long straw an inch from the end.

4 Slide the straws through the holes, carefully working the taped sections through. Insert them so the long one sticks out an inch and the short one sticks out 3½ inches.

5 Set up your fountain: Working at the sink, fill the pint jar two-thirds full with water, then screw on the cap with the straws. Fill the larger jar with water and place it on the edge of the sink as a supply jar.

6 Carefully turn over the straw-topped jar and place the shorter straw in the supply jar. Let the longer straw drain in the sink. The fountain should start to flow.

CONTINUED →

What to Watch For

Look inside the jar. Water should flow out the end of the top straw in a steady stream. Water should also be draining down the long straw into the sink. If you see bubbles rising from where the straws are inserted in the cap, twist the straws to seal them, or remove them and add another layer of tape. If the bubbles come from the edges of the jar lid, screw on the cap more firmly.

What's Going On

The water draining through the long straw lowers the air pressure in the top jar, which causes water to rise up from the supply jar and out the fountain's spout. This is similar to what happens in a siphon, a system where liquids in a tube flow upward a short distance (such as up and over the edge of a bucket), briefly defying gravity. The forces in a siphon work as long as the tube's draining end is lower than its intake end, and the system is airtight. Think of Heron's Fountain as a siphon — but with a water bubbler at its highest point!

Take It Further

Heron's original fountain had additional pipes and chambers that recycled the water, allowing it to bubble for longer periods of time (although not forever, as it might appear). You can find designs for these more elaborate versions online.

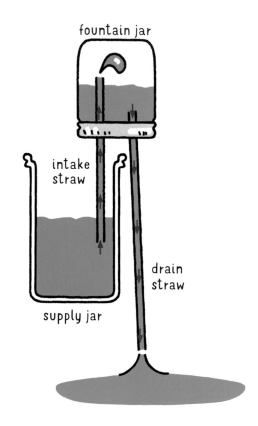

fountain jar

intake straw

drain straw

supply jar

TELL ME MORE

Heron is known for his many remarkable discoveries in math, science, and engineering, but he is also the guy who came up with the world's first vending machine. When ancient Greeks dropped in a coin, they'd get some holy water!

PHYSICS TRICKS

Sometimes a science experiment is successful because it confuses you. What you think *should* happen doesn't, leaving you wondering why. But then, by being forced to think about what's happening, you discover more. These three tricks do just that.

UNSPILLABLE JAR

You may feel some pressure attempting this trick! But thanks to pressure of another kind, you have no reason to worry.

MATERIALS

Pint-size mason jar

A note card or square of stiff paper that's bigger than the jar's mouth

Water

Bucket, large bowl, or sink

INSTRUCTIONS

1 Fill the jar with water. Place the note card over the mouth of the jar.

2 Working over the sink or bucket (just in case!), hold the card against the jar with the palm of your hand and flip both over, so the card is now below the jar.

3 What do you think will happen when you remove your hand? Do it!

What to Watch For

You'd think the water would push away the note card and pour out of the jar, but it doesn't. It just sits there on top of the card. What's holding the water in place?

What's Going On

It may seem like magic, but it's physics. In fact, there are several physical forces at work here. One is the atmospheric or air pressure that surrounds us all the time (for more, see Balloon Barometer, page 55). That force is pressing on the jar and card from all directions, keeping everything in place. For the water to overcome that force and pour out, air would need to flow in to fill the space in the jar, but it can't, because the note card is blocking the opening of the jar. The card is also being held in place by adhesion, the force that makes wet things stick to surfaces, and surface tension, which makes the water want to stick to itself.

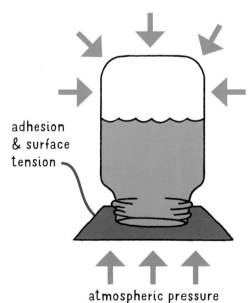

adhesion
& surface
tension

atmospheric pressure

121

BALANCING ACT

Can you get a fork and spoon to balance on the rim of a jar? You sure can, because you have the laws of physics on your side!

MATERIALS

- Pint-size (or larger) mason jar
- Spoon and fork with similar size handles
- Toothpick (preferably one with flat sides)

INSTRUCTIONS

1 Wedge the bowl of the spoon into the tines of the fork (the fork may end up a bit bent). Once they are joined, the two should form a shallow U shape.

2 Insert a toothpick through the middle of the tines of the fork.

3 Set the other end of the toothpick on the rim of the jar, then slowly adjust the fork and spoon and move the toothpick in and out until the whole thing is balanced. Be patient. This may take several attempts!

What's Going On

You've just found the balancing point, or what physicists call the center of gravity, of the fork and spoon assembly. What makes this balancing sculpture look so puzzling is that the balancing point is not a spot on the fork or spoon, but a point *inside* the U shape formed by the two handles. Because the handles are long and heavy, they shift the balancing point to this unexpected location.

Take It Further

To make this demonstration look even more impressive, have an adult light the rim end of the toothpick with a match. The pointed end will burn away but the fire will stop when it gets to the glass rim, leaving the whole assembly balancing on the burnt end of the toothpick.

Unwettable
PAPER TOWEL

An empty jar is not really empty at all, as this simple trick demonstrates.

MATERIALS

Half-pint mason jar

Water

Large bucket,
  bowl, or sink

Paper towel

INSTRUCTIONS

1 Crumple a paper towel into a ball and press it into the bottom of the jar. Make sure the ball stays in place when you turn over the jar.

2 Keeping the jar upside down, submerge it in a bowl, bucket, or sink filled with water.

3 Carefully lift the jar straight out, and check the condition of the paper towel.

What to Watch For

If you kept the jar upright in the water, with the mouth pointed down, the paper towel should be perfectly dry! This has to be magic, right?

What's Going On

Sorry. Once again, it's physics. The jar may look empty, but it's actually filled with air. When you submerge the jar, the air is trapped inside, and water can't get in to wet the paper towel.

SCIENCE IN REAL LIFE

In the days before the invention of scuba diving gear, people used this same trick to breathe underwater, using an invention called a diving bell. The divers would sit or stand inside a huge metal jar that was lowered with ropes into the water. In the 1600s, diving bells were used to salvage treasure from sunken ships, and they were later used for doing underwater repairs on bridges and tunnels.

Edmund Halley, the scientist who discovered Halley's comet, built one in 1691 and tested it in the River Thames. He and five others were able to stay submerged 60 feet down for more than an hour and a half! They brought in fresh air using tanks they lowered from the surface.

GLOSSARY

Adhesion. A force that makes two different substances want to stick together. Adhesion is what makes raindrops, for example, stick to a car window. It's caused by reactions between the electrical charges of the molecules in the water and the glass.

Anthocyanins. A family of pigments that color plants red, purple, or blue. They are found in berries, grapes, eggplants, cabbages, and brightly colored fall leaves.

Aspirator. In entomology (the study of insects), aspirators are mouth-powered vacuums for collecting specimens. They are also called pooters, named for entomologist Frederick Poos, who developed one version.

Atmospheric pressure. Also called barometric pressure or air pressure. Atmospheric pressure is created by the weight of the column of air pressing down on us, roughly 14.69 pounds per square inch at sea level.

Barometer. A device used by meteorologists and others to measure atmospheric pressure. Designs over the years have used water, mercury, and various pressure-sensitive mechanisms to track changes in the weather.

Binomial nomenclature. The system for classifying plants and animals developed in the 1700s by Swedish scientist Carl Linnaeus. Each living thing is given a scientific, or Latin, name, which consists of two parts: the first is the broader group the thing belongs to, called the genus; the second is the more specific subgroup, called the species.

Capillary action. The process by which liquids are drawn into narrow spaces, such as the air pockets of paper towels, the hairs of a paintbrush, or a sponge. Scientists use narrow glass capillary tubes to demonstrate the force, which is caused by the adhesion of liquids to the surface of the small space.

Castings. Earthworm poop, a natural fertilizer that provides important nutrients for plants.

Center of gravity. The point at which gravity pulls down equally on an object, so if you set an object on this point, it would stay balanced.

Crystallization. The process through which a crystal forms, such as by precipitating out of a solution.

Cohesion. A force that makes a substance resist separating from itself.

Colloidal solution. A mixture made up of very tiny particles suspended in water. Quicksand, which is sand suspended in water, is one example.

Condense. The act of a gas, such as water vapor, turning into a liquid, such as water. On a humid day in summer, for example, water vapor in the air will condense into water on the sides of a cold glass of lemonade.

Control. A sample in an experiment that is left unchanged, so you can compare it to the other samples and see the results of your actions.

Copper oxide. The rust-like material that forms on copper when it's exposed to moisture and oxygen.

Cross-linking. The process of connecting the long chains of molecules in a polymer, which causes changes such as making the polymer more stiff or more stretchy.

Density. How heavy something is for its size, or more scientifically, its mass divided by its volume.

Dispersion. The separation of white light into the various colors of the spectrum, as when light is bent through refraction.

Ecosystem. A community of living things that interact within a physical environment.

Evaporate. When a liquid, such as water, turns into a gas, such as water vapor.

Fermentation. The process by which bacteria and other microorganisms break down sugars in food, usually into alcohol, carbon dioxide, and other by-products.

Fixative. A substance that makes pigments more permanent.

Humectant. A substance that keeps things moist.

Hypothesis. A proposed explanation for something, used as a starting point for further research and testing.

Iron oxide. A substance that forms on iron when it is exposed to water and oxygen; rust is one common form of iron oxide.

Lactobacillus. A variety of lactic acid-producing bacteria found in fermented foods such as pickles, sauerkraut, and yogurt.

Larva. The immature stage of insects that go through metamorphosis; caterpillars and grubs are larvae for butterflies and beetles.

Litmus. A dye extracted from lichen that changes color in response to acids or bases.

Magnetoreception. The ability of certain animals to detect the earth's magnetic field and use it to navigate and know where they are.

Malachite. A blue-green compound that forms when copper is exposed to moisture, oxygen, and chlorine.

Metamorphosis. The process by which an animal changes its physical structure.

Osmosis. The movement of a liquid, such as water, through a semi-permeable membrane, such as the wall of a cell, to equalize the concentration of liquid on each side.

Oxidation. A chemical reaction in which a material loses electrons. Rusting is an example of slow oxidation; burning is fast.

Photosynthesis. The process plants use to create food from sunlight, turning water and carbon dioxide from the air into sugar, and giving off oxygen.

Polymer. A material made up of long chains of similar molecules.

Pupa. The stage in the life cycle of an insect that comes after larva, when the caterpillar (or grub, or other juvenile) forms a podlike shell (called a chrysalis in the case of butterflies). After completing metamorphosis, the insect emerges as a mature adult.

Refraction. The bending of light rays (or other energy) that occurs when they pass through different materials.

Saturated solution. A liquid filled with dissolved material to its maximum concentration.

Semi-permeable membrane. A barrier found in cell walls and elsewhere that allows some substances to pass through it under certain conditions.

Sodium chloride. The chemical name for table salt.

Surface tension. The force of attraction that makes liquids bead up and gather in puddles.

Taxonomy. The process of classifying and grouping things, especially plants, animals, and other natural objects.

Transpiration. The process whereby plants draw up water through their roots and release it into the air through small pores in their leaves.

Vortex. A mass of water or air spinning around a central point; whirlpools and tornados are vortices.

Wavelength. The distance between high points in a wave of energy, such as light.

Xylem. The tubelike parts of a plant that carry water up from the roots to the leaves. The tubes that carry food from the leaves to the rest of the plant are called phloem.

METRIC CONVERSION CHART

WEIGHT

TO CONVERT	TO	MULTIPLY
ounces	grams	ounces by 28.35
pounds	grams	pounds by 453.5
pounds	kilograms	pounds by 0.45

US	METRIC
0.035 ounce	1 gram
¼ ounce	7 grams
½ ounce	14 grams
1 ounce	28 grams
1¼ ounces	35 grams
1½ ounces	40 grams
1¾ ounces	50 grams
2½ ounces	70 grams
3½ ounces	100 grams
4 ounces	112 grams
5 ounces	140 grams
8 ounces	228 grams
8¾ ounces	250 grams
10 ounces	280 grams
15 ounces	425 grams
16 ounces (1 pound)	454 grams

TEMPERATURE

TO CONVERT	TO	
Fahrenheit	Celsius	subtract 32 from Fahrenheit temperature, multiply by 5, then divide by 9

VOLUME

TO CONVERT	TO	MULTIPLY
teaspoons	milliliters	teaspoons by 4.93
tablespoons	milliliters	tablespoons by 14.79
fluid ounces	milliliters	fluid ounces by 29.57
cups	milliliters	cups by 236.59
cups	liters	cups by 0.24
pints	milliliters	pints by 473.18
pints	liters	pints by 0.473
quarts	milliliters	quarts by 946.36
quarts	liters	quarts by 0.946
gallons	liters	gallons by 3.785

US	METRIC
1 teaspoon	5 milliliters
1 tablespoon	15 milliliters
¼ cup	60 milliliters
½ cup	120 milliliters
1 cup	230 milliliters
1¼ cups	300 milliliters
1½ cups	360 milliliters
2 cups	460 milliliters
2½ cups	600 milliliters
3 cups	700 milliliters
4 cups (1 quart)	0.95 liter
4 quarts (1 gallon)	3.8 liters

LENGTH

TO CONVERT	TO	MULTIPLY
inches	millimeters	inches by 25.4
inches	centimeters	inches by 2.54
feet	meters	feet by 0.3048
miles	kilometers	miles by 1.609344

High Pressure

 **FAIR**

....
....
....
....
....
....
....
....
....
....
....
....
....
....
....
....
....
....
....
....
....
....
....
....
....
....

CHANGE

 **STORMY**

Low Pressure

Some of the most fun people I know are scientists.
— Mae C. Jemison, astronaut

INDEX

> Science is a way of thinking much more than it is a body of knowledge.
> — Carl Sagan, astronomer

INDEX

All sorts of things can happen when you're open to new ideas and playing around with things.
— Stephanie Kwolek, inventor of Kevlar